Goa

A TRAVELLER'S HISTORICAL AND ARCHITECTURAL GUIDE

front cover: The Church of St Anna at Tallauli

Goa

A TRAVELLER'S HISTORICAL AND ARCHITECTURAL GUIDE

ANTONY HUTT

SCORPION PUBLISHING LIMITED

PUBLISHER'S NOTE

Almost the whole of the text and the selection of the illustrations for this book had already been corrected and prepared for the press before the early and sad death of Antony Hutt in late 1985.

The corrections have been duly incorporated into the text and the illustrations. However, inevitably perhaps, the final presentation of the material has relied greatly upon the enthusiasm and goodwill of many people and friends of Antony Hutt. It is hoped that the work will be seen as a memorial – albeit inadequate – to the author's exceptional and many talents and passion for India, and Goa in particular.

In a draft acknowledgement Antony Hutt recorded his thanks to the officers of the Indian Tourist Office, both in London and India, the Department of Tourism in Goa and many friends in Air India, as well as the Department of Information, the Directorate of Historical Archives and Archaeology, and the Department of Town Planning and Museum in Panjim who provided the plans for the book. Amongst his many friends in Goa he was particularly grateful for the help of Mario, Habiba and Lucio Miranda, Stephen Pereira, the staff of Goa Tours, friends at the Club Nacional and the personnel at the Taj Hotel, Fort Aguada, including Remo Fernandes. Abdul Majeed, Judilia Nunes and Rene Barreto also provided much encouragement. Abercrombie and Kent he thanked for courteously allowing him the opportunity to tour and lecture on his much beloved India. Above all, he wished to thank his parents who provided him with so much support in his endeavours.

The publishers are particularly grateful for the comments of Dr George Michell during the preparation of this book.

NOTE ON SPELLING

In this book the preferences and differences between the Portuguese and Konkani spellings of proper names, and especially placenames, have in general been ignored. The spellings used here have tended to reflect popular usage rather than any theoretical accuracy in pronunciation of spelling. However, the reader and traveller should bear in mind that the main languages in Goa have their own versions of local names.

Text © Executors of Antony Hutt (deceased), 1988

All photos © Executors of Antony Hutt (deceased) except plate 15 courtesy of Department of Information, Government of Goa, Daman and Diu, and plate 31 courtesy of Directorate of Historical Archives.

All plans are courtesy of Department of Town Planning and Museum in Panjim.

First published in 1988 by Scorpion Publishing Ltd
Victoria House, Victoria Road, Buckhurst Hill, Essex IG9 5ES, England
ISBN 0 905906 66 7
Edited by Leonard Harrow and John Orley
Art direction and design: Colin Larkin
Studio assistant: Andrew Nash
Production assistants: Sue Pipe and Kay Larkin
Typeset in Linotype Melior 10 on 12 point
Printed and bound in England by Jolly and Barber Ltd

CONTENTS

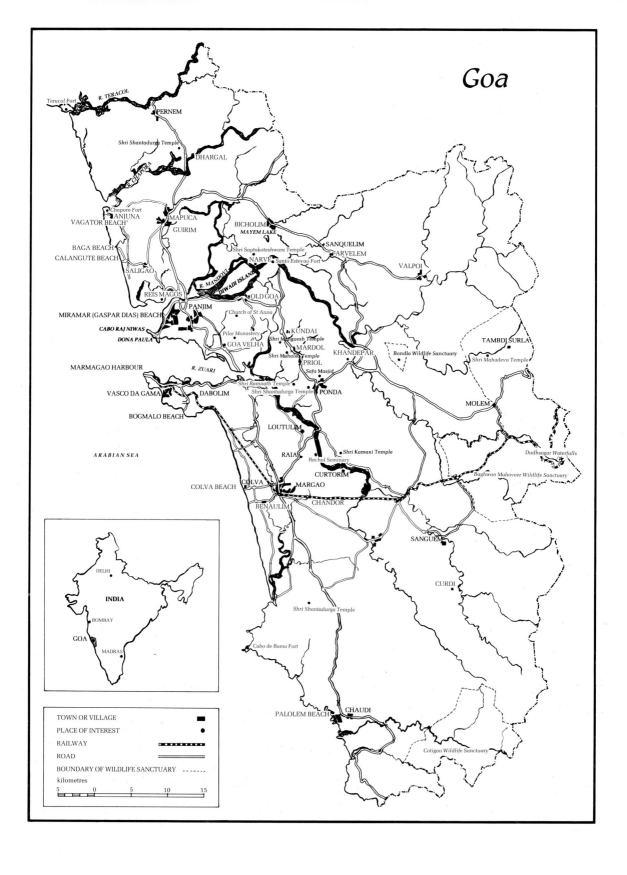

Goa

Teracol Fort
R. TERACOL
PERNEM
Shri Shantadurga Temple
DHARGAL
R. CHAPORA
Chapora Fort
ANJUNA
VAGATOR BEACH'
MAPUCA
GUIRIM
BICHOLIM
MAYEM LAKE
SANQUELIM
Shri Saptakoteshwara Temple
CARVELEM
VALPOI
BAGA BEACH
CALANGUTE BEACH
SALIGAO
NARVE
Santo Estevao Fort
R. MANDOVI
DIWADI ISLAND
REIS MAGOS
OLD GOA
PANJIM
MIRAMAR (GASPAR DIAS) BEACH
Church of St Anna
KUNDAI
TAMBDI SURLA
CABO RAJ NIWAS
Pilar Monastery
Shri Manguesh Temple
Bondla Wildlife Sanctuary
Shri Mahadeva Temple
DONA PAULA
GOA VELHA
MARDOL
Shri Mahalsa Temple
PRIOL
KHANDEPAR
MARMAGAO HARBOUR
R. ZUARI
Safa Masjid
Shri Ramnath Temple
Shri Shantadurga Temple
PONDA
MOLEM
VASCO DA GAMA
DABOLIM
BOGMALO BEACH
LOUTULIM
Dudhsagar Waterfalls
ARABIAN SEA
RAIA
Shri Kamaxi Temple
Rachol Seminary
Baghwan Mahaveer Wildlife Sanctuary
CURTORIM
COLVA BEACH
COLVA
MARGAO
BENAULIM
CHANDOR
SANGUEM
CURDI
Shri Shantadurga Temple
Cabo de Rama Fort
CHAUDI
PALOLEM BEACH
Cotigao Wildlife Sanctuary

DELHI
INDIA
BOMBAY
GOA
MADRAS

TOWN OR VILLAGE
PLACE OF INTEREST
RAILWAY
ROAD
BOUNDARY OF WILDLIFE SANCTUARY
kilometres
5   0   5   10   15

INTRODUCTION

Although small in relation to the immensity of India, Goa has a long and chequered history which goes back through the mists of antiquity and legend, and throughout this long history it has appeared in various guises. In the *Mahabarata* it was known as Gomant, and legend had it that after a particularly wearisome battle, Parasurama, an incarnation of Vishnu, seeking an abode of peace and meditation, shot an arrow from the Western Ghats into the Arabian Sea, and then with the aid of the god of the sea, reclaimed the beautiful land of Gomant.

Lord Shiva himself is also supposed to have stayed in Goa at one time when it was known as Gomantak, at which time seven great sages also performed penance there for seven million years, an event which was so pleasing to the god that he came personally to bless them. The area was also known as Govapuri, and was considered such a blessed place that sins committed in previous existences were destroyed as darkness disappears at sunrise.

In the Hellenistic world it was known more prosaically as either Nelkinda in the *Periplus*, or as *Melinda* in the works of Ptolemy, while later Arab and Persian writers knew it also as Sindabur. To Camões writing in the sixteenth century it was simply 'The Most Illustrious Isle of Goa', the place where he was able to compose his great epic, the *Lusiadas*.

Originally the name Goa was only applied to a small island at the foot of the Western Ghats lying between the Mandovi river to the north, known to the Aryans as the Gomati, and the Zuari River, which the Aryans called the Aghanashini, to the south. The modern names are from Konkani words, *mand* is a tax or toll, and therefore *mandovi* means a toll check post on the river, while *zuar* is Konkani for an island. On the landward side the two rivers are joined by a series of creeks, while to the west the apex of the triangular island divides the estuaries of the two rivers (see map on page 6).

At first the harbour was on the inner reaches of the Zuari, but it was subsequently moved to the north on the Mandovi which connects the present capital Panjim with Old Goa. Modern requirements, however, are somewhat different, and the southern anchorage at the mouth of the Zuari, sheltered by the promontory of Salcete, is once again more important, and the new deepwater harbour of Marmagao has a vital role to play in today's Indian economy.

Over a period of centuries the area of Goa has been considerably extended and its present 120 km coastline extends from the Teracol river in the north to Kanara district in the south. This coastline is broken by a number of navigable rivers which drain the mountain ranges to the east, and whose harbours have helped to make it a flourishing trade centre. Goa now has an area of just over 3,500 sq kms and is divided into 11 talukas or districts; three of these were conquered by the Portuguese early in the sixteenth century and are known as the Old Conquests, while the remaining ones were acquired much later by conquest or by treaty, and are known as the New Conquests.

Inland from the coastal area the territory is hilly, particularly in the New Conquests, and includes a portion of the Western Ghats rising to over 1,000 metres. Generally, however, the land is relatively flat and well-watered so that it is possible to grow a wide variety of products. The climate is pleasantly warm, ranging from a low of 20°C, to a high of 33°C, with rainfall restricted to the monsoon period from June to September.

In recent years large quantities of manganese and iron ore have been discovered, and while the open-cast mining which is being used to extract the ore is aesthetically displeasing and has a bad effect on neighbouring agriculture, income from the export of these products has certainly helped to boost Goa's foreign exchange. Apart from manganese and iron ores, Goa exports only coconuts, fruit and fish, the last mainly salted. Rice is the staple product, and the brilliant green of the paddy fields, fringed with a line of coconut palms among which gleams a white-painted church, is one of the unforgettable sights of Goa. Groves of palms also edge the miles of beaches which are another of the territory's natural beauties, and which form the basis for the current major industry which is tourism.

Tourism is now bringing people into Goa in considerable numbers and has already had an important effect on the general economy. More hotels are being built as well as the basic infrastructure of roads and bridges to link the various parts of the territory, although it is doubtful that events will be allowed to develop to such an extent as to alter radically the character of Goa itself. This is inalienably tied to the character of the people themselves which has evolved gradually over the centuries, tempered by the crosscurrents of history and considerable quantities of palm toddy.

Ethnically the Goans are of mixed descent, which probably helps to account for their charm and attractiveness today. The first inhabitants were probably members of an aboriginal tribe of Dravidian stock who may well have helped to reclaim some of the land from the sea, thus bearing out the Parasurama legend. The fact that the area is mentioned in the *Mahabarata* indicates that it was known to the Aryans, certainly by 600 BC and probably much earlier. One of the Aryan tribal states was the Konkan, of which Goa forms a part, so that this was another area in which the two races would have met.

The word Konkan is still one which has considerable importance in Goa since the area has given its name to the language which is most generally spoken there. Recently, in 1976, this has been recognised by the Central Institute of India for Languages as an independent Indian language. Konkani seems to have derived from an offshoot of Sanskrit which was spoken during the Mauryan period, although there seems to have been no Konkani literature prior to the seventeenth century, and no great literature prior to the twentieth.

It is extremely doubtful that the Hellenistic or Roman traders would have left much of a mark on the ethnic character, but the Arab traders, and the subsequent period of Muslim domination, certainly contributed an element. The mainly Christian Old Conquests naturally also contain a significant proportion of Portuguese blood because of marriages which were not merely tolerated but actively encouraged during the early stages of Portuguese settlement; however, the tradition which tells of Albuquerque asking for Portuguese women to inter-marry with the indigenous inhabitants is probably apocryphal. This complete toleration of mixed marriages has always been a feature of the Portuguese empire, particularly noticeable in Brazil, but for whatever reason over the centuries a distinctive racial type has evolved which is pre-eminently Goan, and is especially famed for its beautiful women.

One of the ways in which this mixture manifests itself is in the cheerful fervour with which members of the various different religions happily celebrate each other's festivals. In addition to the main feasts which are celebrated throughout the Christian and Hindu worlds, there are a number of festivals which are particularly Goan. Many of these are linked to the arrival of the monsoon, the most important single event of the year, since rain has always been crucial to the health of Goa. Other specifically Goan festivals are celebrated by both the Hindu and Christian communities together, such as the feast of the virgin goddess Lairaya, who is also venerated by the Christians as Our Lady of Miracles at the Church of Mapuca in north Goa.

But this intercommunication between the two main religions is not only apparent at festival times. Many of the leading Goan Christian families still maintain the shrines of their ancestral deities which date back to long before the family became Christian. Many of these shrines are outside their original emplacements, particularly in the area of the Old Conquests, having been moved there at the time of religious persecution, but the links are maintained and funds as well as oil and rice are sent to ensure that the shrine is kept in good repair. The caste tradition is also maintained, at least in its major divisions, although its principal manifestation would only relate to marriages.

Thus despite heterogeneous origins, different religions and few clearly defined frontiers, Goa exists as a single unit with a distinctive personality of its own. This has manifested itself not only in the art and architecture of the territory, but also in the general way of life and in the people themselves.

THE EARLY PERIOD

For most people mention of the word 'Goa' conjures up pictures of the somewhat decadent splendour of the sixteenth and seventeenth centuries when the pomp and ceremony of the viceregal court rivalled that of Lisbon and the great city was even compared to Rome. Undoubtedly this was the period of greatest importance for the territory but the Portuguese were not the first to appreciate the strategic value of the area nor of its natural abundance which still conduces to relaxed, indolent living.

Although often concealed by fable and exquisite flights of imagination induced by an almost total absence of documentation, the earlier history of the area can be pieced together, if only as an extension of the history of the south in general. Fortunately occasional monuments do exist which can be used to cover these spare bones with a modicum of flesh and at least provide people with some concrete reminders to enable them to picture the way of life of the earlier inhabitants.

The early prehistoric period of Goan history is completely shrouded in legend and speculation. No archaeological work has as yet been undertaken which would throw much light on this period so that any reasonable hypothesis must stand relatively unchallenged.

According to the most generally accepted theory the arrival of the Aryans in north India around 1500 BC set off a series of chain reactions. The Indus Valley civilisation disintegrated, and the descendants of the highly sophisticated people who had created this civilisation slowly drifted south. At some point in time they entered Goa and mixed with the aboriginal tribes already there, and it was this amalgam which the Aryans found when they eventually reached the area some time before 600 BC.

All of this must remain conjecture, at least until some more concrete evidence is found, but it accords with anthropological and archaeological evidence from the rest of India. Certainly by the third century BC the district of Goa was known and recorded in the annals; it was in fact at this time that Goa entered recorded history.

Like the Aryans before him, Alexander's arrival in India set off chain reactions, and on the ruins of the most easterly Persian satrapy and the northern Indian kingdoms, Chandragupta Maurya was able to found his empire. The expansion and stabilisation of this empire was continued under his son Ashoka until, after a particularly bloody battle which set the seal on his conquests, he decided to consolidate peacefully. He therefore embraced Buddhism with its message of peace, and proceeded to propagate it throughout the empire.

Since Ashoka was undoubtedly one of the most politic as well as one of the wisest of rulers, he fully understood the advantages of a peaceful religion for his government, and so pursued his missionary aims with considerable zeal and fervour. Not only did he erect columns with his edicts engraved on them as well as engraving them on any other vacant columns and rocks he came across, but he also sent out a series of monks to teach the faith all over the empire and indeed beyond it.

At this time Goa rejoiced under the beautiful name of Aparanta, which apparently means 'Beyond the End', and formed one of the provinces of the empire. As part of his missionary work Ashoka sent a Buddhist monk named Puna to proselytize the south, and undoubtedly Goa, along with the rest of the empire, acknowledged Buddhism, although some form of animism probably continued. A number of rock cut sanctuaries and the remains of several statues testify to the continued existence of Buddhism in the region over a considerable period of time although it was probably restricted to court circles.

Ashoka died in 232 BC and the Mauryan empire collapsed almost immediately and split into a number of different kingdoms—a situation which was to continue. The area of the Deccan, including the Konkan, fell to the Andhras also known by their family name Satyavahanas, while the main power in the north went to the Sunga dynasty. After 70 BC however, the Andhras completely supplanted the Sungas and ruled as 'Lords of Dakshinapata', or the Deccan, until they were finally overthrown about 200 AD. Both Pliny and Ptolemy knew of them and referred to them as a powerful nation.

For the next few hundred years Goa does not appear in any of the texts as a separate entity but its history can be deduced by looking at various developments in southern India as a whole. The Andhras themselves had their capital in eastern India while the area of the Konkan was ruled by a governor in a town called Banavasi to the south of Goa. Banavasi was also referred to by Ptolemy who knew it as an important city.

Meanwhile a number of invaders moved into India from the northwest including some of the descendants of Alexander's armies from their Hellenistic Bactrian kingdom in what is now Afghanistan. Some of these moved down into the south and at one time, one group known as the Sakas managed to oust the Andhras from the Konkan for a brief period around 78 AD but they returned and succeeded in retaining their position of supremacy in the south until after the death of the last great Andhra ruler in 196 AD.

After the fall of the Andhra empire there succeeded a period of political instability with a number of small kingdoms making an appearance before the Gupta empire managed to engulf most of northern India in the early fourth century. At about the same time the Pallavas made their appearance as successors to the Andhras in the south and soon consolidated their hold on the Deccan from their capital at Kanchi. While not directly responsible for the Konkan at this time, the Pallavas were at least indirectly responsible for the foundation of the most important Konkani dynasty.

At the beginning of the fifth century a young Brahmin from the Karnataka was sent to study at the Pallava capital Kanchi and while there apparently fought with some of the Pallavas and was forced to flee the city. His subsequent guerilla attacks against the kingdom eventually became so forceful that the Pallavas agreed to an alliance and the young Mayuravarman was appointed military ruler over the lands from the Arabian Sea to Malwa.

From this position he was easily able to establish his independence and founded the Kadamba dynasty which was to rule the Konkan for several centuries. The date of this independence must be about 420 AD because near Belgaum a record of one of the Kadamba kings has been found which was written when he was only the Yuvaraja or annointed successor around 500 AD. In it reference is made to the 'eightieth glorious year', meaning since the foundation of the dynasty, which was done by Mayuravarman, the great-grandfather of the king.

Unfortunately there are no further records of this era because, at some time during the sixth century, the whole of the Deccan once again came under unitary rule with the rise of the early Chalukyas. Having conquered Banavasi and the other Kadamba domains, the remaining Kadambas were content to act as local chieftains under the Chalukyan kings. During the next few centuries the Konkan slumbered peacefully under its various rulers while the Chalukyas and Pallavas fought in the south and when a new power appeared, which defeated the last Chalukyan emperor in 752 AD, the Konkan, along with the rest of the Chalukyan empire, soon submitted to the victorious Rashtrakutas. Apparently this dynasty originated in the region of Goa because they called themselves 'Lords of Lattalura town', which has been identified with Loutulim in southern Goa.

The Kadamba family continued to wield certain authority and was recognised as a royal family because at the beginning of the ninth century we read of a Kadamba princess marrying the Pallava king Dantivarman. However, by the middle of the tenth century, when the Pallava power had been replaced by that of the Cholas, the ruling Rashtrakuta gave the governorship of Banavasi, along with various other ones, to his brother-in-law, thus depriving the Kadambas of one of their main power bases.

In consequence, when a descendant of the former Chalukyan dynasty managed to overthrow the Rashtrakutas in 973 AD and re-establish Chalukyan ascendancy in the Deccan for the next two hundred years, one of the Kadambas seized his opportunity. During the ensuing disruption he decided to restore the fortunes of the dynasty and took control of Gove, or Gopakkapattana, modern Goa, which he ruled as Shastadeva I. From this point in time can be dated the existence of Goa as a separate political entity distinct from the rest of the Konkan.

As the Chalukyas consolidated their hold on the Deccan all the various minor states acknowledged their supremacy. The south Konkan was actually ruled from Banavasi by the sister of one of the Chalukyan rulers, but the Kadambas were left in peace to govern Goa while recognising the Chalukyas as suzerain. The Kadamba princesses were also apparently still greatly in demand as much for their intelligence as for their beauty, a granddaughter of Shastadeva married the Ruler of Gujarat and even acted as Regent for her son for a time. This obviously became a tradition because some hundred years later a similar situation arose and the Kadamba princess again acted as Regent. During this latter period Gujarat was invaded by the Muslims under Muhammad Ghuri in 1178 prior to the eventual conquest of Delhi. Queen Naikidevi 'taking her son in her lap', led the Gujarat army against the Muslims and defeated them at Gadaraghatta near Mount Abu, thus adding heroism to the other qualities of the Kadamba ladies.

During the later Rashtrakuta period the Konkan had been governed by a dynasty called Silahara, and it was against this dynasty that Shastadeva had rebelled and gained his independence. The Silaharas had ruled Goa from Chandrapura, modern Chandor, and Shastadeva continued to use this town as his capital. An inscription from the time of Shastadeva describes the town as being a very pleasant place in which to live, and it was certainly an area which had already begun to attract a considerable amount of international attention.

The deep-water natural harbours of Goa had long been recognised by traders, and in particular by the Arabs. From ports in southern Arabia they sailed in one direction along the whole coast of East Africa, and in the other around India to South East Asia and even on to China. Along the Indian coast their main ports were in Gujarat, Goa, and Calicut, and these ports provided important points of entry for all the goods which they were bringing to India. A number of these Arab traders settled in parts of India, acting presumably as agents and merchants.

Despite the Muslim-Turkish invasions of India from the northwest, and the considerable destruction of Hindu temples and way of life which this involved, the Arabs were actively encouraged by the various coastal rulers both to trade and to settle. At this stage there was no question of persecution from religious motives in the minds of the Hindu rulers, and certainly no mental link was made between the urbane Arab traders and their apparently barbaric co-religionists to the north. Jayasimha Siddharaja of Gujarat (1094–1143) punished some of his subjects for interfering with the worship of the Muslims, and subsequently Sarangadeva of Gujarat (1294–97) gave a grant for a mosque to the local community of Prabhasa Pattana.

The advantages of Goa's harbours were not only appreciated by foreign traders, Shastadeva himself had a powerful fleet which he apparently sent as far as Ceylon to levy tribute from 'the grim barbarian tribes'. This was in fact a period of great naval expansion for India. In the south the Chola empire was the first great Indian kingdom to recognise the importance of naval power, and the Bay of Bengal became a Chola lake, while their colonial empire embraced Ceylon, the Nicobar Islands, the Malay Peninsula, and Sumatra. It was also a period in which the influence of India was extremely widespread, particularly in south-east Asia where Hindu kingdoms were established in many places including the Sailendra empire in Malaya, the Khmer empire in Cambodia, the Champas in Indo-China, and the kingdoms of Java which eventually shrunk to the island of Bali which still exists as a Hindu island in Indonesia. All of these countries naturally looked towards India as their lodestar and trade between them was considerable, in all of which Goa was superbly placed to play an important role.

Under Shastadeva's son Jayakeshi I, Goa profited considerably from all this trade, and the capital was moved from Chandrapura to the north bank of the Zuari river nearer to the great harbour. The city was called Govapuri or Gopakkapattana, and was on the site of present day Goa Velha. It was apparently a very beautiful and well laid out city which greatly impressed all the visitors with the wealth and power of the Kadambas who flourished considerably in association with the Chalukyas. At times the Kadambas tried to assert their independence but this only resulted in fairly swift retribution, as when Govapuri was burnt down by order of Vikramaditya VI after a minor revolt, but all soon returned to amity and Vikramaditya's daughter was married to Jayakeshi II who ruled Goa from 1125 to 1147. This was obviously a good marriage because Jayakeshi then had other parts of the Konkan added to his domains which he ruled jointly with his queen as a subordinate of the Chalukyas.

This alliance with the Chalukyas did not however prevent Jayakeshi II allying himself with the growing power of the neighbouring Hoysalas, and at one point, around 1135, rebelling against his brother-in-law. This rebellion was also swiftly terminated, although on this occasion Govapuri was not destroyed and Jayakeshi seems to have been restored to favour.

The Chalukyas eventually succumbed to the Yadavas, another Deccan dynasty, and it is interesting to note that the last Chalukyan ruler, after his defeat in 1189, took shelter with the Kadamba Jayakeshi III, who acknowledged his suzerainty at least up until 1198 when he presumably died. The next hundred years saw the Deccan divided between the Yadavas and the Hoysalas, and Jayakeshi III's son Tribhuvanamalla soon found it politic to submit to the Yadava Singhana, a position in which they remained until the Muslim invasion of 1310 finally shattered the Yadava kingdom along with most of the other southern powers.

During all this period Goa prospered and traded not only with the neighbouring states but with all the different countries and nationalities who were attracted by the riches of the Indian market. One of the most important articles of trade was horses, and these were imported from Arabia, usually entering India via Goa. Many of these horses were destined for the great Chola empire in the south and to the successor Pandyan kingdom. Marco Polo visited the Pandyan kingdom around 1293 and described the arrival of the ships from Hormuz, Kish Island in the Gulf, Aden and all Arabia, laden with horses and other things for sale. However, he pointed attention to the speedy death of most of the imported horses owing to the absence of farriers and general mismanagement with consequent colossal financial loss.

Govapuri grew as a city with temples and palaces and even charitable institutions founded by the Kadambas, the copper foundation plaque of one of which survives to tell that the charity was paid for by levying a tax and customs duty on the foreign community of traders. However, nothing survives of Govapuri itself and only one major Kadamba temple remains in all of Goa to show the architectural glories of the period, a small Shiva temple dedicated to Shri Mahadeva at Tambdi Surla (*col. pl. 1*) on the eastern border of the territory. This very beautiful temple is a superb example of Kadamba-Chalukyan architecture and can be dated to the twelfth or thirteenth century, and its very fine stone carving gives some idea of the vanished splendours of Goa under the Kadambas.

The temple faces east and is situated in dense forest on the bank of a small river (pl. 1). It is raised on a plainly moulded plinth and consists of a main hall (sabhamandapa), a middle hall/vestibule (antaralaya), and a sanctuary (garbagriha), each following the other on a principal axis. The main hall (pl. 2) has three projecting entrances facing north, east, and south, each approached by a flight of steps. There are ten plain pillars with simple mouldings on the sides and four well-carved pillars in the central bay of the main hall. There are four niches for statues in the rear walls, and the other open sides of the main hall have sloping stone seat-backs. The ceiling over the side bays is made up of large sloping slabs of stone, while over the central bay there are a series of reducing tiers finally covered with a rectangular slab beautifully carved with lotus reliefs (pl. 3).

The doorway of the vestibule is flanked by perforated grilles while the doorway of the sanctuary has a decorated lintel. The exterior walls are plain except for a series of rosettes carved in bold relief around the lower portion of the main hall. The spire (shikhara) above the sanctuary has a number of niches ornamented with a series of bas-reliefs of superb workmanship (pls. 4–5). These include statues of Brahma, Vishnu, Shiva, Parvati, and Kalabhairava as well as one of an elephant trampling a horse which probably has political significance.

1 The Shri Mahadeva temple at Tambdi Surla

A number of features including the ground plan, the shikhara, the carvings and the style of the pillars, in particular the knife-edge moulding below the actual capital, have a close relation to the western Chalukyan or Yadava temples as well as to the Hoysala styles and would therefore agree with a twelfth or thirteenth century date for the temple.

Another small Shiva temple at Curdi in Sanguem taluka seems to be of a similar date to Tambdi Surla, that is from the eleventh to the thirteenth century, and is therefore also Kadamba. It is however much smaller than the Tambdi Surla Mahadeva temple and only consists of an entrance hall/vestibule (antaralaya) and a sanctuary (garbagriha). The carving and general architectural details are in a similar style, although in a much more damaged condition.

There are several groups of rock cut sanctuaries in Goa most of which are probably Buddhist in origin. The earliest would seem to be a group of six caves near the Arvelem waterfall (*col. pl. 2*), estimates of their age ranging from the third to the sixth century AD. The caves were all carved into a single stone outcrop, but are divided into two groups, each group having a common portico onto which the

2 The interior of the mandapa of the Tambdi Surla temple

3 A detail of the lotus motif ceiling of the mandapa

4 The shikhara of the Tambdi Surla temple

5 A detail of the carving on the shikhara of the temple

individual caves open. Each of the caves is quite small and devoid of any architectural detail except for a very simple altar block which presumably originally supported a statue of the Buddha. At some comparatively early time in their history the Arvelem caves were converted to Shiva worship, and each of the altars is now graced with a Shiva lingam set within a small pit excavated into the stone.

None of the Arvelem caves is large enough, or has any indication that they were used as living quarters for monks, whereas the cave complex at Rivona undoubtedly formed a habitation. The lower outer cave has a large porch overlooking a small pool and garden area, and leads back into a central vestibule. This contains a well with abundant water, above which a funnel-shaped dome leads to a small roof opening. A finely architected doorway leads into an inner room which has been carved from the rock in a fairly exact manner, while a secondary doorway opens onto steps and a sloping passage which leads to the upper level. This is a large cleared open space with the appearance of some form of amphitheatre, the natural stone at the rim having in some instances been carved into benches.

While the major part of the cave has been hollowed out of the living rock, some parts of it have been built up out of blocks cut from the same stone. Archaeological evidence suggests that the complex dates from the seventh century AD and was certainly Buddhist in origin. Subsequently it was converted, as were the Arvelem caves, and the outer porch now boasts a number of small carved stones including one with an image of Hanuman (pl. 6) having the long curved tail reminiscent of Vijayanagar carvings and similar to a sixteenth century example from Khandepar now in the Archaeological Museum in Panjim.

One other very interesting group has recently been discovered which can also be assigned to this period. Near Khandepar four free-standing rock cut sanctuaries (*col. pl. 3*) have been carved out of a hillock which stands some fifty metres from a local tributary of the Mandovi river. Like all the other Goan caves these have been carved from the coastal laterite formations which, being a soft stone, easily lends itself to rough shaping with simple instruments and only requires a chisel for the finishing stages.

Caves one and two are carved from a single block and have an outer and inner cell as does cave three which is adjacent to cave two at one metre distance. The fourth cave which is single-celled, is sited immediately opposite cave one at a slight distance. Each of the caves was fitted with a tiered roof in temple spire (shikhara) form, but the major part of this was not integral with the caves being built up of laterite blocks laid on top of the main structure.

These rock cut sanctuaries are the finest in Goa and undoubtedly the best equipped. Sockets were provided for wooden doors and there are even the remains of schist frames on some of the inner doorways. Pegs were also carved out of the rock for hanging robes, and a number of niches of varying sizes were provided which could have been used for storing lamps and other belongings. The outer cell of cave one also has the form of a lantern ceiling with a central lotus motif carved into the ceiling in imitation of contemporary temple structures, and it can be assumed that this cave probably formed the home of the leader of this small monastery.

6 Vijayanagan carving of Hanuman at the entrance to the Rivona cave

The single-celled cave number four which faces the other three was not provided with any of this extra detail and probably formed the temple or meditation room of the complex.

On the basis of the design of the shikara and the use of the lantern-style roof the caves can be dated to the tenth or eleventh centuries, and therefore can be considered Kadamba monuments and were probably Buddhist in origin although they may have been taken over at a later stage like the other caves.

Buddhism certainly had a continued existence in Goa and was sufficiently noticeable in the eleventh and twelfth centuries to be referred to by the Sanskrit writer Hemachandra who, referring to the court of the Kadamba king Jayakeshi I, mentions Buddha Jatis (Buddhist monks) talking to the King of Chandrapur. An image of the Buddha was discovered in the last century by the historian Fr. Heras at Mushir near Colvale, and this seems to be an eleventh century image similar to one at Anuradhapur in Sri Lanka.

The only other remains from the early period of Goa's history are a number of images of the gods, many of them still in worship, the remainder either in the museums or in remote parts of the jungle. During the period of the Inquisition all the temples and mosques in the Old Conquests were destroyed, but the majority of the images were saved and removed to areas outside Portuguese jurisdiction. When those areas were subsequently incorporated within Goa the power of the Inquisition had waned and the images were allowed to remain in peace and in fact formed the nucleus for a series of new temple buildings which are now one of the glories of Goa.

One image, that of Navadurga at Madkai, is said to have been established in 1150 by Kamiladevi, a Kadamba queen, and at approximately the same time the royal family apparently adopted the Saptakoteshwara form of Martanda-Bhairava as their family deity. The name of this god was often inscribed on Kadamba coins, and during the religious persecution by the Bahmani kings between 1356–66, the lingam of Saptakoteshwara was hidden by his devotees. This was re-established in 1391 under the rule of Vijayanagar, but the temple at Narve was destroyed in 1560 by the Portuguese and the remaining main dome transformed into a chapel. The lingam was however saved and the present temple at new Narve in Bicholim was reconstructed in 1668 at the orders of Shivaji, the founder of the Maratha empire, after he had conquered the area.

It had taken a major defeat to convince the Kadamba Tribhuvanamalla that he should accept the suzerainty of the Yadavas, and his successor who ruled from 1246 to 1260, met with an equally stern response when he evinced similar pretensions. By the time Kamadeva came to the throne in 1260 the lesson had been thoroughly learned and the Yadavas were accepted as overlords of the whole region.

After fifty fairly uneventful years of rule, Kamadeva was to see the entire balance of power in the south totally upset by the advent of a great Muslim army, sent like some avenging thunderbolt from the Sultan of Delhi. With this began a new era for Goa, one in which she was to be invaded repeatedly for some two hundred years, culminating in her capture by the Portuguese who were to inaugurate the most brilliant period in her history.

THE PERIOD OF INVASIONS

While Muslim Arab traders had been building a commercial empire along the southern coasts of India, other Muslims had been pouring into northwestern India with vastly different ideas. In the late tenth century Mahmud of Ghazni made a series of devastating yearly raids into northwest India.

These initial raids had two main themes, the destruction of the temples and shrines which Islam associated with idolatry, and the acquisition of immense quantities of wealth from these same sanctuaries and the various defeated peoples. After Mahmud the raids became a more permanent settling; Delhi was made the capital, and the Sultanate of Delhi became the focus for Muslim rule.

It was in 1296 that 'Ala ud-Din Khalji made his first expedition to the south and it was desire for more southern gold that caused him to send his General Malik Kafur on a second expedition in 1307. In 1310 he returned to Delhi with treasures too heavy for a thousand camels to bear. At the end of 1310 he once again set out for the south and devastated most of the Pandyan kingdom eventually returning in 1311 once again weighed down with immense quantities of treasure and a record of innumerable temples sacked and destroyed.

By 1320 there had been a change in dynasty and Ghiyas ud-Din Tughluq was on the throne, which was shortly followed by the inevitable expedition to the south in search of treasure. This expedition, and a second one in 1323, were both led by the Sultan's son Prince Jauna Khan, who in 1325, after the death of his father in somewhat questionable circumstances, ascended the throne under the name Muhammad bin Tughluq, or Muhammad Shah.

One of the most interesting characters to sit on the throne of Delhi, Muhammad bin Tughluq's first acts had to do with putting down the rebellion of one of his family in the south. An army was immediately despatched and by 1328 his authority was established over most of India almost up to the southernmost extremity. In order to facilitate his control over the south he moved the capital from Delhi to Devagiri, which he renamed Daulatabad. This move was not carried out without considerable hardship, and many of the population of Delhi who were forcibly removed from their houses, died on the journey, and when eventually after ten years they were all sent back, again at the decision of the Sultan, hardly a third of the original inhabitants were left after this forced migration.

The fact that Muhammad bin Tughluq was able to carry out such a decision testifies to his amazing character, which is amply borne out by the description of him given by the famous writer Ibn Batutah. Nothing was allowed to stand in his way, although he was also capable of the greatest generosity and understanding towards those people whom he appreciated.

While there are no specific records in the chronicles about either Malik Kafur or Muhammad bin Tughluq having visited Goa in person, nor of their having despatched armies against the state, there is a very strong tradition of the sack of Goa at this time, and when the great Ibn Batutah joined the expedition against Sandapur, as Goa was called in the Arabic texts, he refers to a previous conquest of the city. The absence of any specific reference in the detailed accounts of Malik Kafur's campaign may be a strong indication that he was not involved in Goa, but Muhammad bin Tughluq's armies were in the south for a considerable period of time, and during any of these manoeuvres a detachment could have been sent to subdue Goa which was by this time an important port on the western coast.

A further possibility is that the Arab traders themselves may well at some time have actually taken over the town. Many of the traders were men of considerable substance, having several ships, all of which would have been armed against pirates. The presence of Arab traders is attested at an early stage, in fact Gopakkapattana owed a substantial part of its prosperity to the wise administration of the Arab merchant, Chhadama, who was the minister of Jayakeshi I. Chhadama also built a mosque in the city for the benefit of his community, and in 1053 Jayakeshi made certain monetary concessions for its maintenance. In the early part of the fourteenth century a merchant named Hasan built a congregational mosque at Sandapur, as attested by Ibn Batutah, and it was this same Hasan who had a disagreement with the ruler and was forced to leave the city. It may well have been some attempt at control which caused the break, but the eventual consequences were certainly unfortunate for Goa.

Hasan and his family migrated south to Honavar, also on the coast, and by the time of Ibn Batutah's visit in 1343 his son Jamal ud-Din, was recognised as Sultan of Honavar. He was apparently a powerful local prince, who was able to field at least 6,000 troops as well as a reasonably sized navy, although he found it politic to pay tribute to the newly created Hindu Empire of Vijayanagar which was subsequently to play such an important role in Goa's history.

The loss of their position in Goa was obviously still remembered with regret, and when the son of the Kadamba ruler, after a quarrel with his father offered to betray the city, become a Muslim, and marry the Sultan's sister, Jamal ud-Din was not slow to react. Assembling his forces he attempted to take the city, but was repulsed the first day. The second day he was able to use his secret weapon—two vessels with open sterns in which were horses. These ships were built in such a way that the cavalry was able to mount inside and come out riding, with the result that the local forces were defeated and the Kadamba ruler was forced to flee the city.

Jamal ud-Din installed himself inside the palace, and having pardoned the populace, assigned the remaining ten thousand of them to a suburb of the city and settled down to rule. We have an interesting eye-witness account of this whole operation in that the Sultan took along Ibn Batutah who happened to be visiting Honavar at the time, and who has left us a record. By the beginning of 1344 Ibn Batutah had decided to move on to another site, but he returned to Goa some six months later and found the city besieged by the returning Kadamba. He just managed to effect his escape before the city fell, but apparently Jamal ud-Din was not so lucky because other chroniclers recall that the rulers of Honavar suffered so much as the result of an expedition to Sandapur that they never recovered their former state.

This incident shows that much of the fighting along the coast was done independently of the happenings either in Delhi or the Deccan, although any major happenings there were bound to have an effect on the area. Two events which were to have particular importance for Goa were the creation of the Muslim Bahmani kingdom and that of the Hindu empire of Vijayanagar to which allusion has already been made. Although the Vijayanagar empire was founded in 1336 it did not immediately come into contact with the Kadamba state whereas it seems probable that Goa and the Konkan coast were annexed to the Bahmani kingdom during the reign of the first king.

In 1345 a rebellion broke out in the south against Muhammad bin Tughluq, and although he defeated the rebels in open conflict, their leader and a number of others managed to shut themselves into the great fort at Daulatabad, which the Sultan promptly settled down to besiege. Unfortunately another rebellion broke out in Gujarat and he was forced to raise the siege and march north to deal with the new problem. The Sultan died in 1351 having been unable to return to the south, and in fact this area became permanently lost to the Delhi Sultanate. In the meantime Abu 'l-Muzaffar 'Ala ud-Din Bahman Shah was able to be crowned king of Daulatabad in 1347.

While the exact date of the conquest of Goa by the Bahmanis is not recorded it must have been before the death of Abu 'l-Muzaffar which occurred in 1358. By that time he controlled the ports on the Konkan coast and the passes leading to them from his new capital which he had sited at Gulbarga.

It was at this period that the first Bahmani persecution of Hindus took place, as has been mentioned above. Apparently a very sharp distinction must be drawn between the Muslim Arab traders who had been settled on the coast for generations, and their co-religionists who had moved into India through Afghanistan and the northwest. The coastal traders had been living among the Hindus for a considerable period of time, mosques had been built and they had enjoyed the favour of some of the rulers to such an extent that the rulers had supported their rights to practise their religion in peace, and in many instances even made grants towards the construction of mosques. An attitude of mutual tolerance therefore already existed on the coast between the two communities; any internecine wars between the various kingdoms were purely political without any concomitant religious persecution. When Goa was captured by Honavar, the ten thousand Hindu inhabitants were simply moved from the central town, having been pardoned, and settled in one of the suburbs, and even this had no suggestion of religious conflict but was a purely political distinction.

With the arrival of the Muslims from the northwest, the 'Turks' as distinct from the Arabs, events took a very different turn. The first raids into India on the part of Mahmud of Ghazni had been with the announced intention of destroying the temples of the idolators, and this conception had permeated the invading Muslims' thoughts ever since. The fourteenth century saw the appearance of this spirit of fanaticism in the south for the first time. It is small wonder that the people of the south had paid little heed to the extraordinary tales of destruction which must have trickled through concerning events in the north: they knew the Muslims, having lived with them for centuries, and did not appreciate that they were dealing with an entirely new spiritual force which was essentially intolerant.

The forces of Malik Kafur deliberately devastated whole areas with their destructive force particularly concentrated on the temples, which, in addition to their idolatrous content were also the main repositories of the wealth of the area so that there was an added incentive. The armies of Muhammad bin Tughluq were similarly motivated with similar results as far as the local population was concerned, and the Bahmanis continued the same tradition. For the people of Goa this had the result that for the first time it became necessary to conceal the important images of the gods, and, as has been mentioned above, the linga of Saptakotisha was hidden by his devotees during this period. Unfortunately, once having been introduced to the area, the spirit of fanaticism took a long time to die out, and atrocities committed in the name of religion were to continue. Eventually they reached their peak under the rule of the Inquisition which was introduced after the Portuguese conquest, although as yet all of this was hidden in the future, only the first blows had fallen.

As has already been mentioned even in 1343 the Sultan of Honavar had deemed it politic to pay tribute to the king of Vijayanagar, so that at this stage some sort of overlordship was acknowledged, but by 1358 certainly a major part of the Konkan acknowledged the rule of the Bahmanis. In 1378 the Bahmani Sultan Mujahid was assassinated while returning from a war with the king of Vijayanagar, and during the dissensions which followed, including the assassination of his successor, Vijayanagar was able to wrest a large slice of territory on the western coast including Goa. This event is referred to in a copper grant of 1391 in which the chief city of the Konkan is referred to as Gowa or Gowapura, and which mentions the reconquest of Goa from the 'Turushkas' meaning the Turks or Muslims.

The Vijayanagar Governor of Goa was Madhava Raya and he was able to organise a further conquest of the remainder of the Konkan in a campaign which lasted from 1387 to 1395.

Madhava Raya was also a great Vedic scholar and he was concerned to re-establish the Hindu traditions which had been interrupted by the Bahmani interregnum. One of his major acts was the reconstruction of the shrine of Saptakoteshwara and the re-installation of the lingam which had been hidden during the Bahmani period. In addition to this he also revived the tradition of Vedic and Puranic learning by laying the foundation of Brahmapuris, colonies of Brahmins, in at least three places within the territory of Goa. One of these was made by the amalgamation of two villages on Goa island on the site which subsequently became Old Goa, so that already the Mandovi was also being investigated as a development in addition to the estuary of the Zuari. This Brahmapuri at Old Goa was on the site of a previous one founded, according to some copper laminates dated 1107, by King Tribhuvana-Malla, and was probably dispersed during the Bahmani period.

The significance of the Mandovi at this time under the Vijayanagar empire is borne out by the village of Ribandar which is a small town on a hill overlooking a natural harbour on the river. The name in fact means the harbour of the rayas, or kings, and refers to the kings of Vijayanagar. This would seem to imply some shift of emphasis from Gopakkapattana during this period although there is no record of the capital having been moved.

1 The Shri Mahadeva temple at Tambdi Surla

3 One of the free-standing rock cut sanctuaries at Khandepar

2 opposite: Early rock cut cave shrines at Arvelem

4 *The Safa mosque, Ponda*

5 *The Church of Our Lady of the Immaculate Conception in Panjim*

7 above: New paddy fields

6 opposite: Our Lady of the Immaculate Conception, showing detail of the facade

9 Palm trees on a beach at sunset

10 A cove at Anjuna beach

16 The interior of the Chapel of St Anthony

17 A lone fisherman on the Teracol river

19 *Fishermen on Calangute beach*

20 *The interior of the dome of the Church of St Cajetan*

23 Pilar Seminary, Goa Velha

During this entire period wars continued between the Vijayanagar and Bahmani kingdoms with both sides being fairly evenly balanced. In this naturally Goa acted as one of the main ports for the Vijayanagar empire, particularly for the importation of horses from the Gulf. These horses of course came from the Islamic world and were destined to help a Hindu kingdom in its wars with a Muslim state, but this was a nicety of religious distinction which was not made at this time. Further, while both armies destroyed mosques and temples as appropriate, this spirit did not extend as far as people themselves were concerned.

Events continued in this way until in 1469 the then king of Vijayanagar, Virupaksha Raya II, moved against the Muslims of the Konkan in a singularly thoughtless fashion. In addition to Goa, one of the other ports on the coast used for the importation of horses was Bhatkal, and these were imported by the considerable Muslim colony settled there. Some of these horses were also being sold to the Bahmanis, and in 1469 Virupaksha getting angry at this, ordered his vassal in Honavar to kill as many Muslims as possible and drive the rest away. In the subsequent slaughter some ten thousand are said to have lost their lives, and the remaining survivors fled and settled in Goa. This provided the excuse for which the Bahmanis were looking, and they accordingly attacked to save their co-religionists.

In 1425 Ahmad Shah Bahmani had moved his capital from Gulbarga to Bidar, and it was to this court in 1453 that the most remarkable figure of the age first appeared. Mahmud Gawan was originally a merchant from Persia who had first appeared in Dhabol and then made his way to Bidar where he entered the service of the Bahmanis and where his exceptional talents soon made themselves felt. His rise was rapid and by 1461 was a member of a three-man Council of Regency for the young king, and by 1466 was Chief Minister with the title Vakil us-Sultanat (Deputy of the Kingdom). He was to remain in supreme authority until his death in 1481. During this time he brought the whole of the Bombay-Karnatak under Bahmani sway, and also subjugated the Konkan and captured the port of Goa which Gawan himself described as the 'envy of the islands and ports of India'.

The excuse for the attack on the Konkan having been provided by Virupaksha, Khwaja Mahmud Gawan gathered troops from various areas and attacked the Konkan in 1469. He was held up for five months at the fortress of Vishalghad, but it eventually capitulated and Gavan was free to attack Goa. In 1470 he sent 120 ships to attack by sea while he marched with the army. His attack was so swift and successful that before Virupaksha could send any reinforcements the territory had fallen and the Muslims were again masters of Goa. The news was so well received in Bidar that the king ordered triumphal music for seven days as well as other rejoicings; history does not record Virupaksha's reactions.

The Muslim army, perhaps in retaliation for the slaughter of their co-religionists, seem to have utterly destroyed Gopakkapattana, and moved the capital to the village of Ela on the Mandovi. This was on the site of the Brahmapuri founded by Madhava Raya in the previous century and followed the tradition already established of transferring interest from the Zuari to the Mandovi. Under Muslim rule Ela developed into a considerable city and the Mandovi throve as a harbour for the trade which had once filled the coffers of Gopakkapattana and Chandrapur.

In the meantime within the Bahmani kingdom dissensions had occurred which were to have important consequences and eventually to split the kingdom.

24 The monumental cross at Margao

By 1490, in fact if not in name, the Bahmani Kingdom had ceased to exist and had been replaced by five Sultanates, the Qutb Shahi of Golconda, the Nizam Shahi of Ahmednagar, the Barid Shahi of Bidar, the 'Imad Shahi of Berar, and the 'Adil Shahi of Bijapur. Goa and the territory of the Konkan, came within the power of Yusuf 'Adil Shah, ruler of Bijapur, and in fact Goa was considered the second city of his kingdom and the brightest jewel in his crown.

In Ela itself Yusuf 'Adil Shah built a splendid palace, now almost totally destroyed, only the fragments of a stone doorway remaining to testify to the grandeur of the design (pl. 7). These fragments are carved in basalt and, because of their figural content and design must have come from a Hindu temple or shrine, probably a temple attached to the Brahmapuri of Madhava Raya. The palace was a magnificent two storeyed building with three arched entrances and lofty staircases which was referred to by travellers at the time of the Portuguese conquest as being the most conspicuous building in the city. After the conquest it was used by the Viceroys and Governors until 1695, although in 1560 the court of the Inquisition was also stationed in the palace which thereafter came to be called the Palace of the Inquisition. To the Portuguese at the time of the conquest it was known as the palace of the Sabaio, that being their name for the 'Adil Shah.

7 A section of the carved basalt doorway of Yusuf 'Adil Shah's palace showing the Hindu-style carving

8 The Secretariat building in Panjim, formerly the 'Adil Shah's palace

In addition to the palace a number of other buildings were erected including a fort and at least one mosque. Although all trace of these has disappeared some idea of the scope and style of building may be gauged by reference to the Jami' Mosque which Yusuf 'Adil Shah built in Bijapur. In comparison with the later magnificent buildings of Bijapur this is a modest structure although having considerable elegance. The sanctuary facade has three arched openings and is only one bay deep and fronts onto a small courtyard. The dome already has the high drum and slender petal-shaped merlons associated with the later Bijapuri style, while the minarets are purely decorative, the call to prayer presumably being given from the roof.

Although it is possible that Goa being an important commercial entrepôt might have disposed of larger funds than Bijapur, the inland capital of the young state, Ela itself was only a recent foundation and it is unlikely that the congregational mosque of Goa would have been much larger or very different from that constructed at Bijapur. The refugees from Bhatkal would also have required housing and a mosque and it is possible that this structure might have been different from that erected by Yusuf himself and subject to different cultural influences, but one must assume that Ela at this time presented the picture of a thriving port with essentially single storeyed houses for the most part, an occasional mosque but without high minarets, and the Palace of Yusuf 'Adil Shah rising above all.

In addition to developing the town of Ela, Yusuf also built himself a summer palace at a small village called Panjhe nearer to the mouth of the Mandovi. An inscription of 7 February 1107 refers to Pahajani Kali, and describes some charitable deeds of the Kadamba governor of the region, so that the village had a long history prior to the Muslim presence. The two-storeyed palace also acted as a fortress and, at the time of the Portuguese attack in 1510, was defended by fifty-five pieces of artillery. The river originally came to the foot of the building so that people could embark directly, and was further defended by a saline creek which flowed alongside.

After the Portuguese conquest the palace continued to be used and eventually became the palace of the Governors after the capital was moved to Panjim. A number of modifications were made to it during the succeeding centuries although the original building was apparently comfortable enough judging by the description of 1608 when Pyrard wrote that the fort 'had good living rooms which form a beautiful and comfortable palace, where the Viceroys land when they arrive from Portugal'. In 1613 considerable changes were made, as in 1887 and 1900, but in essence the palace retained its basic shape, and today it houses the Secretariat (pl. 8), so that the Palace of Yusuf 'Adil Shah still remains at the centre of Goan life.

Events stood thus along the coast when in 1498 a new group of people arrived in India for the first time. After a voyage of some ten months Vasco da Gama and his small flotilla of ships had arrived in India from Portugal and the age of European involvement in the East had commenced.

THE ARRIVAL OF THE PORTUGUESE

In the Mediterranean world the fifteenth century is notable for a number of significant events. Early in the century it saw a resurgent Christendom successfully attacking Islam within its own territories when Portugal, which had expelled the Moors from her own territory in 1249, in 1415 captured and retained the North African port of Ceuta. By the end of the century Islam had also been totally expelled from Spain, and the crusading zeal which had accomplished this seeming impossibility was looking for fresh outlets.

While Columbus's famous voyage of discovery tends to overshadow all other explorations, the Portuguese, under the initial impetus of Prince Henry the Navigator, had also been slowly expanding European knowledge down the west coast of Africa, and by 1488 Dias had successfully rounded the Cape of Good Hope. This memorable event set the scene for Vasco da Gama's epic voyage to the Indian Ocean which finally brought the Europeans into Asia en masse.

The fifteenth century also saw the appearance of the Ottoman Turks as a major Mediterranean power, conquering most of the Balkans by the middle of the century, and by its end having rounded out their conquests with the capture of Constantinople. By the middle of the sixteenth century they had extended their rule through Syria and Egypt, into Iraq and as far south as Aden, so that not only did the Ottomans face the monolithic might of the Hapsburg Empire across the Mediterranean but they also became involved with the Portuguese sea-borne empire in the Indian Ocean.

From this turmoil it is interesting that it should have been Portugal, with comparatively few resources either of manpower or finance, which became the first of the European powers to establish an overseas empire, and which was to retain it for the longest. It is also interesting to examine the motives behind this sudden expansion, motives which were to colour the subsequent history of expansion and the way in which the resultant empire was governed.

Undoubtedly the most potent force behind this expansion was the crusading zeal against the Moors. Although they had been expelled from Portugal in 1249, their continued presence in the Iberian Peninsula acted as a permanent irritant spurring the Portuguese to further action, the first result of which was the capture of Ceuta. By extension this feeling against the Moors was taken to include all Muslims and subsequently, as the empire expanded, was directed against any non-Christians which was to have particularly savage results in Goa.

The other reasons behind this expansion were the desire for Guinea gold; the quest for Prester John, the semi-legendary Christian ruler whom the Portuguese hoped would ally with them against the Muslims in a pincer movement; and lastly the quest for Oriental spices. Eventually the latter was to become almost as powerful a spur as the crusading motive, and at times deliberations of trading profits were able to exercise a moderating influence on the excesses of religious fervour.

Throughout this period the navigators whom Prince Henry trained at Cape St Vincent were meticulous in their observations so that the maps which they had inherited from the Arabs and Jews were continually augmented and substantiated. Information was also fed into the voyages of exploration by travellers who were sent overland to the east, as for example Pero de Covilha who left Portugal in 1487 and reached India. He apparently had good information about the Indian Ocean which he sent back to Portugal before he continued to Ethiopia whose ruler was identified with Prester John, and where he remained for the next thirty years. In this way when Vasco da Gama eventually left in 1497 he carried with him reasonable maps as well as a certain amount of information about his destination.

At the time of da Gama's arrival the Indian Ocean was almost as coherent an area as the Mediterranean, with an extremely strong link between East Africa and India. In much of this area the trade had also changed hands and the Arab traders had in many places given way to Indian Muslim traders, who continued to spread Islam in Africa by the peaceful means of marrying local wives to look after them during their long stays away from home. At first the Portuguese arrival was merely noted and accepted as bringing more trade into the area, with no ripple of unease as to the eventual outcome, although the Portuguese ships were obviously immensely more powerful than anything else in an area where none of the bordering empires, Egyptian, Persian nor Vijayanagan maintained any warships.

Da Gama sailed along the African coast, visiting a number of ports and making copious notes before acquiring the famous Muslim pilot Ibn Majid in Malindi on the East African coast and sailing directly across the Indian Ocean for twenty-three days before eventually docking at Calicut. Tradition has it that on landing some of the Portuguese were taken to a nearby temple, probably that of Mari, goddess of smallpox, and, under the impression that the Indians were Christian, assumed that it was a shrine to the Virgin Mary and consequently made their devotions and gave thanks for a safe landing, to the evident approval of the local Brahmins. The local Muslim traders however were under no illusions as to the importance of the arrival of the Christians in south India, and two Tunisian traders who could speak Castilian and Genoese, greeted them with: 'May the devil take thee! What brought you hither?'

Letters and presents were eventually exchanged with the ruler of Calicut and da Gama sailed home with information that caused King Manuel to write jubilantly to Ferdinand and Isabella of Spain announcing the successful discovery, and also to the Papacy requesting confirmation of his own overlordship of the Indian Ocean. This latter was particularly important as showing his intentions to legalise the Portuguese presence in the area, and at the same time it signalled the first split in the Venetian-Muslim monopoly of the Levant trade in spices and Asian luxury goods, although the eventual loss to Venetian trade may be regarded as a consequence rather than a major reason for the voyages. At this stage the exact location of the Christian kingdom of Prester John was not clearly fixed and a clear title to the entire Indian Ocean would enable the Portuguese to ally themselves to any Christian potentate in a combined attack on the Muslims.

The next expedition was sent in 1500, and although at first the Portuguese were well received by the ruler of Calicut, the Muslim traders were by now thoroughly alarmed and managed to infect the ruler with their fears. As a result the fleet sailed to Cochin and on to Cannanore and established good relations with the respective Rajas who were both feudatories of the ruler of Calicut and saw this as a good opportunity of asserting their independence. Having established a factory in Cochin as a base, the Portuguese fleet sailed home with considerably more information.

A second fleet, once again commanded by Vasco da Gama, appeared in 1502, and strengthened the factory at Cochin and erected a defensive palisade at Cannanore. When da Gama sailed home he left a small fleet to patrol the coast which was eventually supported by three further squadrons, one of which was commanded by Afonso de Albuquerque. Having once again assisted the Raja of Cochin against the ruler of Calicut, the Portuguese were able to build their first fortress in India at Cochin, which then became their main base, and when Francisco d'Almeida arrived as the first Viceroy, he made Cochin his headquarters.

The destruction of a fleet of Muslim traders which had been armed and equipped by the ruler of Calicut, seriously alarmed all the Muslim states bordering the Indian Ocean since it signalled the growing strength of the Portuguese. In 1508 a combined Egyptian-Gujarati fleet managed to sink a few Portuguese ships, including one carrying d'Almeida's son, but this success was not to be repeated, and in 1509 the Viceroy avenged his son's death by inflicting a crushing defeat on the combined Muslim fleet off Diu on the coast of Gujarat. After this he set out for Portugal leaving Afonso de Albuquerque as his successor as Governor of India, but unfortunately died on the return journey.

Although the Muslim fleet had been defeated it had not been totally destroyed, and had in fact limped into Goa where it was being refitted preparatory to another attack on the Portuguese. Albuquerque knew that the fleet had not been destroyed but assumed that it had managed to regain the Red Sea, and accordingly in February 1510 set out to find it, having sacked Calicut as a gesture against the Muslim traders, completely unaware that his enemies were in fact so close at hand.

Fortunately for the Portuguese Albuquerque put in at the port of Karwar on his way north and there met a sea captain in the service of Vijayanagar. To the Portuguese he was known as Temoja, but his real name was Timmaya and he came from Hunnawar, and since relations between the Portuguese and Vijayanagar were amicable, Timmaya was only too pleased to be able to give them more correct information. Relations between the two powers had been cordial from the beginning, and when d'Almeida had first appeared as Viceroy, Vira Narasimha Raya II had immediately despatched an ambassador with presents and an expressed wish to increase trade between the two countries, an offer which also included the king's sister as prospective bride for the Prince of Portugal. Nothing seems to have come of this offer, but at least relations were friendly and some sort of treaty was concluded.

Vira Narasimha died in 1509 and was succeeded by his brother the great Krishna Deva Raya under whom the Vijayanagar empire reached its greatest extent. At the beginning of 1510 Albuquerque sent a Franciscan friar, Fray Luiz, to Krishna Deva Raya proposing an alliance against the Muslims both in Calicut and Goa, and promising a monopoly in the trade in horses from Hormuz. At that time Vijayanagar was at peace with Bijapur and the king therefore only returned a general answer, but again indicated his good will towards the Portuguese.

It was thus only natural that Timmaya should have fallen in with Albuquerque's proposals for a combined attack on Goa which would result in the destruction of the Muslim fleet and the loss of the finest port of the rulers of Bijapur. The exact final disposition of Goa after its conquest seems to have been less carefully decided, although Timmaya was under the impression that he was going to retain it in return for an annual payment to the Portuguese. Albuquerque's initial intentions may indeed have been to carry out this agreement, but these certainly changed after he saw the place, and he soon realised that this naturally defensible island would make a perfect base for the Portuguese empire and the foundation for his own Governorate of India, so far merely an almost empty title.

Timmaya appears to have entered into relations with the Hindus of the city to ensure that they certainly stayed neutral, and when the Portuguese fleet arrived at the end of February 1510 they were able to take the whole area virtually unopposed. Having first captured the palace of the 'Adil Shah in Panjim, the way was open to the capital Ela, and the defenceless city was surrendered to Albuquerque by eight of the leading Muslim citizens in return for a number of guarantees on both sides.

While the Portuguese were consolidating their conquest, Yusuf 'Adil Shah died and was succeeded by his thirteen year old son Ismail, known subsequently to the Portuguese as Idalcan to distinguish him from his father who had been known as the Sabaio. The Regent for the young ruler was Kamal Khan, the Chief Minister, and they were not slow to react to the loss of one of their fairest cities. Swiftly assembling an immense army mainly composed of veterans from the continual wars with Vijayanagar, the Muslim leaders launched an attack which the Portuguese were not long able to withstand. They managed to hold off the Muslims for a few weeks but eventually were forced to re-embark and the city was once more in the jubilant hands of the 'Adil Shah.

Unfortunately for the Portuguese it was the rainy season and the monsoon rains pinned the ships inside the mouth of the Mandovi where they pitched helplessly for three months, short of food and under constant cannon fire from the fort at Panjim which they had also been forced to evacuate. Eventually the weather improved and Albuquerque was able to recapture Panjim fort and then take the battered remnants of his fleet, firstly to the island of Angediva and then on to Cannanore. While in Cannanore he learnt that Ismail 'Adil Shah and his Minister had returned to Bijapur where they were occupied with ensuring the peaceful takeover of the state and had left Goa lightly defended. Armed with this information Albuquerque was able to commandeer a fleet of ten ships newly arrived from Portugal en route for Malacca, and with this sizeable addition to his forces, returned to Angediva to plan the reconquest of Goa.

Having explained the situation to his enthusiastic captains, Albuquerque once again sailed up the Mandovi and, after reconnoitring the newly erected defences of Ela, finally attacked the city on St Catherine's day, 25 November, 1510. The attack was totally successful and within hours resistance was over so that Albuquerque was able to re-enter his island fortress, this time knowing that he had sufficient forces to prevent its loss a second time.

The Muslim population had either been forced to flee across the backwater channels or had been killed in the fighting, so that after the battle there remained only the Portuguese, their allies, and the Hindu population, and with these helpers Albuquerque set about reconstructing the city along more European lines. 'Adil Shah's palace became the residence of the Governor, and a church, dedicated appropriately to St Catherine, was built opposite to serve as the nucleus of the new Christian town.

However, the most immediate need was for improved fortifications to ensure that the Muslims could never recapture the city. A new fort was built in European style with a two-storey keep for artillery and square towers at the corners, dominating the city and the river. The ramparts were also rebuilt using whatever stone was available including the stones from the Muslim cemetery.

All of this was done with extraordinary speed, everyone including the officers being required to labour at the building, and by the time Albuquerque left in April 1511, the new colony was considerably more prepared for the inevitable counter-attack from the Idalcan, which occurred promptly as soon as Albuquerque had left. Despite the loss of the garrison commander, the city managed to survive the rainy season and reinforcements arrived soon afterwards. Albuquerque himself returned from his successful expedition to the East in late 1512 and immediately attacked and captured the fort which the Muslims had built at Banastarim and from which they were besieging the city. By annexing this fort and rebuilding it, he made Goa sufficiently safe and was able to leave on further expeditions to enlarge the Portuguese possessions.

Not content with the conquest of Goa, Albuquerque added Malacca to the Portuguese empire in 1511, and the subsequent capture of Hormuz in 1515 gave Portugal almost complete control of the major entrepôts and thereby of the total Indian Ocean trade. The one failure which can be attributed to Albuquerque, despite an attempt in 1513, was his inability to capture Aden and thus close the Red Sea to the spice trade in the same way that the capture of Hormuz had closed the Gulf. This failure was to enable the Ottomans subsequently to obtain a foothold in the area and so disrupt the Portuguese trade monopoly; Albuquerque's first intimation of the growing Ottoman power however reached him in a curiously roundabout manner.

Pero de Covilha's sojourn in Ethiopia had apparently been successful because the Empress Eleni, who was acting Regent for her grandson, decided to send an embassy to the King of Portugal warning him of the Ottoman menace and proposing an alliance to be cemented by marriages between the two Christian royal families. Because of a similar Monophysite tradition the Ethiopian and Armenian churches had a long background of mutual support, in particular the richer Armenian church was very helpful to the Ethiopian community in Jerusalem, the Empress therefore naturally chose an Armenian as her envoy from her land-locked kingdom to the outer world. Matthew set out in late 1509 laden with letters and gifts for the Portuguese monarch, including a jewelled cross containing a fragment of the True Cross, and eventually arrived in Goa shortly after its final conquest. Prester, or perhaps more correctly Presbyter John, had not merely been discovered he had sent envoys bearing rich gifts, and thus another of the original Portuguese aims had been fulfilled.

Albuquerque and the entire clergy came down to the ship to escort the envoy and his precious relic, and, despite certain misgivings among some of the officials who could not understand why an Ethiopian monarch should send a non-Ethiopian ambassador, Matthew was eventually sent on to Portugal with every mark of respect. In Lisbon he was received by the King and even went to Rome for an audience with the Pope before returning to Goa in 1515 as guide for the Portuguese return embassy to Ethiopia. Due to various delays, including the death of the Portuguese ambassador, they did not finally reach Ethiopia until 1520, and the longed-for treaty failed to materialise. The Empress was no longer Regent, and the Portuguese failure in the Red Sea, coupled with undoubtedly prejudiced information from India via Muslim traders, made the new Emperor less than enthusiastic, so that Albuquerque's grand design of an alliance between Ethiopian manpower and the Portuguese navy to crush the Muslim powers in a pincer movement was completely lost.

However, contact had been made between Goa and Ethiopia and while this certainly helped the development of East African trade it also almost inevitably led to the eventual establishment of a Jesuit mission in Ethiopia. At one stage this mission had such a success that in 1622 the Emperor Susneyos publicly submitted to Rome, but such an important success led to an equal reaction and under the next ruler the trend was completely reversed and the Order was expelled in 1634. This also had the effect of souring relations with the Portuguese empire already engaged in a major struggle with the Dutch. The Ethiopians were also apparently aware of this shift in the power structure in the east and in the latter half of the seventeenth century they sent another Armenian envoy, Murad, first directly to the court of Aurangzeb in Delhi, and then subsequently to Batavia, the capital of the Dutch East Indies. This latter was so successful that Murad eventually made three trips in 1673, 1689 and 1692, thereby signalling a complete change of alliance away from the crusading mission of the Portuguese Catholics.

Ethiopian doubts about the value of a Portuguese alliance in 1520 were to be justified shortly afterwards when the events which the Empress Eleni had foreseen actually occurred, and the Portuguese were unable to prevent them. Had an alliance between the Portuguese and the Ethiopians existed it is doubtful whether it would have altered the course of events, and might simply have alerted the Ottomans to the existence of Ethiopia with disastrous consequences, instead of which it was allowed to develop undisturbed by the Turkish advance to the north.

After the Ottoman capture of Syria and Egypt, the Ottoman governor, Suleyman Pasha, at his own initiative, had a navy built at Suez and sailed thus to the Indian Ocean conquering Aden and the Yemen on the way in 1530–31. In 1535 some of the Muslim rulers of India were becoming increasingly aware of the Portuguese menace, and an embassy was sent to the Ottoman Sultan Suleyman the Magnificent requesting aid against them. The embassy included Bahadur Shah, ruler of Gujarat; however, after the return of the embassy but before the promised aid could be sent, Bahadur Shah was assassinated and Mahmud III installed as ruler, while the Portuguese occupied the port of Diu which was to remain part of the territory of Goa.

In June 1538 Suleyman Pasha sailed from Suez with 20,000 men, 7,000 being Janissaries. He reached Gujarat in August and besieged a number of forts including

Diu, and invited Mahmud III to join him. The Portuguese resisted successfully, and Suleyman Pasha returned to Aden at the end of the year. The Turkish sources declare that he returned with much booty which may well have accrued from attacks on Portuguese shipping or on some of the pirates which also infested the Indian Ocean at this time, but in any case it demonstrated that the Ottomans had an interest in the areas which they intended to maintain.

The Red Sea remained a Muslim lake and the capture of Aden gave the Ottomans a window onto the Indian Ocean which was of considerable importance for trade. Despite the Portuguese hold on Diu and Hormuz, Gujarati ships were still able to evade the blockade and to unload considerable quantities of pepper at Jeddah whence it either went directly into the Ottoman empire or was transhipped through Egypt to the Mediterranean as before.

Although Albuquerque defeated a Javanese warfleet off Malacca in 1513 further eastward expansion was always difficult because of the strength of the Chinese, and in fact Portuguese vessels were defeated in both 1521 and 1522 by Chinese coastguard fleets, and they only eventually penetrated the Chinese trade on Chinese terms. Macao was founded in 1557 which completed the main chain of Portuguese colonies and ensured them the control of the spice trade west to Europe. East of Macao the Spanish empire controlled the trade across the Pacific to their own conquests in South America and then onwards to Europe, but the hegemony of the Portuguese from the Indies westward to Europe via the Cape was never seriously disputed during the sixteenth century.

By far the brightest jewel in this empire and the seat of the Viceroys was 'Golden Goa', which Albuquerque insisted on retaining despite initial misgivings from the court in Lisbon. The crusading zeal which had successfully captured the island from the Muslims was not however to be satisfied merely with conquest, the other side was now to be revealed, that of conversion to Christianity. By now the Portuguese realised that the Hindus were not in fact Christians and therefore presented a most fertile field for the priests on the various expeditions to plough and sow, and accordingly the Franciscan Friars began to preach.

Albuquerque had certain other ideas as well which he felt would strongly assist the creation of a Christian Portuguese Goa, and this was the intermarriage of his soldiers with the native inhabitants. A new race would thus be created which would have its roots in the soil of Goa but would equally be loyal to the Portuguese crown and thus ensure continuity. Albuquerque himself was not particularly bigoted, although this in no way diminished his zeal for the slaughter of Muslims, but it did enable him to actively encourage these mixed marriages by providing dowries where necessary, and overbearing any misgivings among the clergy.

The temporal needs of these new colonists were further assisted by grants of land to both soldiers and civilians, but the spiritual side was also of considerable importance. The clergy might have genuine doubts about the validity of many of the conversions, but with both parents at least nominally Christian the Church could afford to relax in the certain knowledge that future generations would be brought up in the faith. The majority of other converts were former low-caste Hindus who hoped by changing their religion to escape the laws of caste. This had earlier been the case with both Buddhism and Islam and had always called into question the genuineness of such conversions, but as always the Church obtained control of the children which ensured the future for which she was willing to make certain minor exceptions in the present.

Interestingly enough in Goa conversion to Christianity did not in fact overturn the caste barriers. Later on as more and more people became Christian, for whatever reason, they still retained their caste differentials, and particularly in the case of marriages, caste continued to go with its own caste, although of course the public disabilities inherent in some of the lower castes were no longer enforced. Even today Brahmin or Kshatriya Christians will still know their own caste and native village, and many still send money for the upkeep of the family deity.

Albuquerque died in 1515 and was buried in Goa, although his remains were subsequently disinterred and returned to Portugal in 1556. By the time he died Goa was already firmly Portuguese and on the way to becoming a Christian city. After his death, with his moderating influence no longer in evidence, the rate of conversion was speeded considerably, although still not at the rate it was to attain later on.

One of the main articles of commerce for the port of Goa was the transhipment of horses from the Gulf, embarked at the Portuguese port of Hormuz, and the main market for these was the Hindu empire of Vijayanagar, continually at war with its Muslim neighbours. On the news of the second conquest of Goa Krishna Deva Raya had sent ambassadors to congratulate the Portuguese, but Albuquerque was in Malacca at that time and there had been no reply to this embassy until he returned and sent Gaspar to Vijayanagar in 1512. There were no conclusive results of these embassies, but in 1514 Krishna Deva Raya sent a senior embassy to Goa to arrange for the supply of horses and seek co-operation with the Portuguese in a war about to be waged against the 'Adil Shah. A similar embassy arrived at the same time from Bijapur, and Albuquerque tried to bargain between the two parties, but eventually entered into a pact with Vijayanagar by which the king agreed to pay the wages of the men Albuquerque sent to take part in the proposed war, and to pay 30,000 cruzados annually for horses. Important commercial considerations were therefore at work to ensure that, at least while the territory was being formed and was therefore vulnerable, no major attack was made on the Hindu population which could be interpreted as an attack on Hinduism in general, although this was also to change as the territory was consolidated and the influence of the clergy increased.

Albuquerque's original conquest had been of the island of Tiswadi on which the town of Goa is situated, and along with these he took control of the provinces of Bardez, Salcete and Ponda. The provinces he again lost the following year to a counterattack by the Bijapur forces, but in 1530 they were conquered by Vijayanagar, and relations were so good that they were promptly donated to the Portuguese. Once again the Bijapuris attacked and reclaimed all three in 1533 only to lose Bardez and Salcete to the Portuguese again the following year. Until 1543 there followed a series of attack and counterattack, but after that time they were almost permanently in the possession of Portugal, until after the treaty of 1571 they were definitely integrated into the Portuguese colonial territories. These three provinces, Tiswadi, now called Ilhas, Bardez and Salcete are thus known as the 'Old Conquests' and form the nucleus of the territory of Goa.

The New Conquests, which include the provinces of Pernem, Satari, Bicholim, Sanguem, Ponda, Quepem and Canacona, came into the Portuguese possession considerably later, either by conquest or treaty. The nearby presence of these provinces however enabled many of the Hindus to find shelter there, both for themselves and also for the sacred images which were to be the particular target for the furious Portuguese iconoclasm. By the time that these provinces were eventually acquired there was a much greater spirit of tolerance, and the power of the Inquisition had been broken so that they did not suffer as much as had the original territory.

Unfortunately the central nucleus had always been the richest part of the territory, and the destruction of the temples which began in 1541 in Ilhas, and was then continued in 1567 in the other two provinces, destroyed many great shrines and, judging by the few pitiful remains, superb works of art. Naturally not all of the temples were important or substantial, particularly judging by the numbers quoted – 116 in Ilhas, 176 in Bardez, and 264 in Salcete – but the total destruction of this entire section of Goan life was an immense and cruel loss.

The actual pace of conversion slowly began to increase, and by 1534 there were sufficient Christians for the Pope, Paul III, to constitute Goa a separate diocese, and in 1538 the first Bishop, Juan de Albuquerque was installed. In 1558 it was raised to an archdiocese which for centuries held pride of place in the East and whose prelate also bore the proud title 'Primate of All India'. Earlier, in 1532, Miguel Vaz had arrived in Goa as Vicar General, and he was a particularly zealous Christian, anxious to eradicate all traces of any other religion in the territory. With the aid of the bishop and the first Jesuits who arrived in 1540, Vaz was able to have a first law promulgated on the subject in June 1541 which declared that the king had ordered the destruction of all the temples on Ilhas, and Vaz set to with such relish that he even forced the Hindus to destroy their own temples. All of the temple properties were then listed, confiscated and handed over to the Church.

Not content with this Vaz returned to Portugal in 1545 and placed a similar plan before the king for the newly acquired provinces of Bardez and Salcete. As a result of this Vaz returned to Goa with the king's agreement in 1546, and in March of that year a 'Carta Regia' was published which formally ordained that idolatry should be eradicated in Goa by dismantling the temples, forbidding the festivals, exiling the Brahmins, and severely punishing anyone caught making an idol of wood, stone or metal. With this carte blanche behind him Vaz went to work and within a very short space of time he had fundamentally accomplished the major part of this programme of destruction.

More was to follow. In 1557 non-Christians were excluded from public office; in 1559 it was forbidden to have idols in private houses; and in the same year all orphans were entrusted to a Judge of Orphans who sent them to the College of St Paul. In 1560 it was decreed that all Brahmins were to be expelled from the lands of His Majesty and sent to the galleys, and also in 1560 the Tribunal of the Holy Office, the Inquisition, was established in Goa.

Under the wave of persecution that followed, those who could fled to the lands of the neighbouring provinces, later to be the New Conquests, and as a result commerce and agriculture declined at an alarming rate, to such an extent that one of the Viceroys attempted to entice them back by decree of immunity, but the Church represented this as prejudicial to Christianisation, and the decree was declared null and void. Further decrees and laws followed making the lot of the

Hindus even worse, until by the early seventeenth century, with the exception of essential services such as farmers, carpenters, blacksmiths, and notably doctors, all Hindus were forbidden to live within Goan territory.

Into this maelstrom in 1542 came St Francis Xavier, the Conqueror of Souls. Avoiding the Viceregal pomp which had been prepared to greet his arrival, the saint walked ashore and wandered around the territory in a completely unpretentious manner. Approached by Miguel Vaz and another priest, who had founded a seminary called the College of the Holy Faith, Xavier agreed to become a teacher there and remained for almost a year before moving on to continue his missionary work. Before the end of 1542 he was much further south on the Fishery Coast where he remained for two years in which time it is estimated that he baptised 30,000 people. These local pearl fishers had accepted Portuguese protection against the Muslims, but these latter feared the loss of their pearling industry if the Christians were too successful and had attacked the converts. This had resulted in a Portuguese fleet being despatched which had a decisive victory over the Muslims in 1538, so that, by the time that St Francis arrived peace had been restored.

After moving east to Malacca to continue his work there, St Francis was inspired to continue to Japan and accordingly he and three Japanese first returned to Goa to prepare for the expedition, and then in 1549 left for Japan. His mission there was important as sowing the seeds for subsequent missionary work in Japan, but he himself returned to Malacca to prepare for another expedition to try to enter China. In this he was finally unsuccessful and died in 1552 on a small island off the Chinese coast having been unable to obtain entry to the empire. His remains were first buried on the island, but then disinterred and taken to Malacca and eventually back to Goa where they now form the principal treasure of the territory.

While these events were taking place in the territory of Goa other events involved her also in affairs of the Deccan and South India. Ibrahim 'Adil Shah had ascended the throne of Bijapur in 1534 and had alienated a number of his nobles to such an extent that a party was formed to place his younger brother Prince Abdullah on the throne. The conspiracy being discovered, the prince fled to Goa where he was well received by the Viceroy. This however incensed Ibrahim who attacked the Portuguese but eventually made a treaty whereby he ceded Bardez and Salcete along with a certain amount of treasure in return for the dismissal of the prince to a place where he could no longer disturb the peace of Bijapur. The Portuguese merely sent the prince to Cannanore and then brought him back to Goa where offers of the cession of the entire Konkan should he ever become ruler, contrived to keep the Viceroy firmly on his side.

After Ibrahim sent more than one expedition to attempt to regain the provinces he had ceded, the Viceroy, Garcia de Castro, made defensive treaties with both Vijayanagar and the Nizam Shahs of Ahmednagar in September 1547. For the Portuguese this was an important treaty in that it gave Vijayanagar the monopoly of the horse trade of Goa in return for defense against Bijapur and an agreement that all Vijayanagan merchants would trade through ports where the Portuguese had factories, none being permitted to proceed to Bijapur. Shortly after this Abdullah did apparently march out of Goa with Portuguese help and proclaimed himself ruler, but the rebellion was unsuccessful and the Portuguese eventually returned to Goa taking the prince with them. After this they concluded a more satisfactory treaty with Bijapur which patched things up for a while.

In 1555 the Portuguese again supported Abdullah in rebellion and successfully took Ponda which became the seat of his government. At this time Vijayanagar was in alliance with Bijapur and the 'Adil Shah therefore sent for aid to Vijayanagar and the joint army attacked. Abdullah was eventually made a prisoner and the Portuguese were forced back to within their own boundaries, but not before capturing quantities of booty and ships and reducing Dhabol and many Bijapuri villages to ashes. Peace being sought by both sides a fresh treaty was drawn up which temporarily ended hostilities.

In 1559, partially in retaliation for a Vijayanagan attack on the Christian community on the east coast near Madras, the Portuguese sacked Mangalore and a number of other ports along the Malabar coast. Despite these various incidents however, trade with Vijayanagar was most important to the continued success of Goa, and the destruction of the empire in 1565 was a blow which, coupled with the increasing religious bigotry and persecution, was a major cause of the decline of the territory.

Ibrahim 'Adil Shah had died in 1557 and had been succeeded by his second son 'Ali, and it was he who in 1564 first proposed a league among all five Shahi rulers against Vijayanagar. Only by agreeing among themselves and uniting the territories which had once formed the great Bahmani empire could they be successful against the Hindu empire. At the battle of Talikota in January 1565 this indeed proved to be the case and the Vijayanagan army was totally destroyed and the great City of Victory itself was ruthlessly sacked and plundered. So enormous was the city that the sack lasted for more than six months, and the loot was so great that each of the Shahi rulers was able to adorn his capital with a magnificent series of buildings – certainly the glory of Bijapur dates from this point. After the destruction however the unifying effect of a common enemy was removed and fighting soon broke out between the Muslim states, which was to continue in varying ways until they were all absorbed by the relentless southward advance of the Mughal Empire.

In addition to the superb array of churches which still remain and which will be discussed at length, Goa possesses one other interesting survivor from this period, the Safa Masjid in Ponda (col. pl. 4). Ponda was not officially taken by Goa until it was ceded by the King of Sunda in the Treaty of 1791, but it had been one of the first provinces originally conquered by the Portuguese at the time of the capture of Goa by Albuquerque. It was lost again almost immediately to Bijapur, but at the time of Prince Abdullah's rebellion in 1555 it was again captured and it was in Ponda that Abdullah set up his government. When the allied Vijayanagar-Bijapuri forces attacked they were once again able to retake Ponda, and it was shortly after this, in 1560, that the mosque was constructed by 'Ali 'Adil Shah who had succeeded his father in 1557, possibly as part of a plan to underline the Bijapuri control over the area.

The mosque itself is a single rectangular chamber with a pointed roof, a protruding mihrab, and a built-in minbar. It is set on a high, solid plinth with a flight of steps. The whole rests on a low platform, on the outer edges of which are the remains of a number of octagonal columns. If the pitched roof were to be extended to cover the platform area, resting on the columns, the style of the building would be in the local vernacular and would provide a protection against the monsoon rains. The detailing and ornamentation in the architecture accord with the Bijapuri style (pls. 9–10) before its great development after the capture of Vijayanagar, while the pitched roof and high plinth would accord with local climatic considerations.

The mosque is unusual in having a large rectangular water tank on the south side (pl. 11), whereas most ablutions tanks would have been placed at the front on the eastern side. The ornamentation accords with that of the mosque itself and it would appear that they are both contemporaneous. There is a local legend that it is dangerous to swim underwater in the tank because of the possibility of getting lost in the tunnels surrounding it. The existence of some other exit is borne out by a smaller tank which is situated nearby and apparently linked to the main tank.

While the mosque is a lone reminder of the non-Christian sixteenth century architecture of Goa, the glories of Golden Goa, even in their present ruined state, are still awe-inspiring. The riches which once poured in to erect these great churches and monasteries, soon ceased to flow, but during a comparatively brief time there was not only sufficient money but also sufficient belief and ardour to create a major European city on the Mandovi whose wild life and beauty astonished the visitor. Seeing some of these monuments dreamily emerging from the surrounding jungle is sometimes sad because they seem to demand a pulsating life around them, but it can still create a sense of wonderment that they exist there at all.

9 The interior of the Safa mosque with the Bijapuri-style arches

10 An exterior detail of the Safa mosque showing the carved laterite mouldings

11 The Safa mosque, Ponda, showing the large adjacent tank

GOLDEN GOA

In the sixteenth and early seventeenth centuries Goa was one of the wonders of the world, with an estimated population of about 300,000 plus a floating population of seamen, merchants and travellers. Larger than Lisbon or London it was fed by an annual migration from Portugal which maintained the city's population, periodically decimated by disease and epidemics, at the cost of leaving much of Portugal itself untilled.

The drain on Portuguese manpower was enormous. Out of an estimated population which never rose above 1,500,000, some 2,500 emigrated annually, and of these many died in the long and arduous voyage to the east. This compares with an annual emigration of 1,000 from Spain with an estimated 7 or 8 million population and a much shorter voyage across to the Americas. An acute shortage of manpower and shipping were the two great problems of the extended Portuguese empire, and eventually these problems became so acute that when the other European countries finally emerged into the Indian Ocean Portugal was unable to prevent them seizing the major and richer parts of the area. Those colonies which remained to Portugal were eventually forced to rely on their own human resources and, as trade and therefore employment declined in Goa, the tables turned and in the end her greatest export was the Goans, who spread themselves throughout the Portuguese-influenced world and beyond, industriously sending money back to Goa.

All this however was in the future, and at the time of her greatest prosperity, Goa acted like a magnet drawing all towards herself. Situated at the hub of a network of short and medium range routes which actually encompassed almost every coast of Asia, the city was closely interlinked with local conditions of supply and demand. Commerce developed throughout the Indian Ocean, and journeys to Macao and Japan yielded easily as much as the long journey home around the Cape which probably accounted for no more than a fifth of the total profits pouring into the city. The Cape route was in fact at times a loser since there was no demand for Portuguese products in the east and they were obliged to pay in precious metals for the spices they acquired. The City's merchants however swiftly adjusted to this economic environment and, using native associates as their commercial advisers, quickly grasped the trading ideas of their precursors so that the trading wealth of the entire area was soon diverted into Goa.

In 1534 the Portuguese had acquired Bassein, a town near Bombay, also originally Portuguese but which was given to the English as part of the dowry of Catherine of Braganza when she married Charles II in 1662, and it was from Bassein that Goa was able to draw upon splendid supplies of limestone. This Bassein limestone was finely grained, almost like marble, and quantities of it were used to build the shining churches and palaces of Goa.

Unfortunately the shining buildings rose out of a mire c
the city surrounded by stagnant marshes which formed the
millions of mosquitoes and other insects, but also the sanitatio.
much to be desired, even by the standards of that time. The .
epidemic occurred in 1543, and thereafter regularly until by
eighteenth century, after a number of previous abortive attemp.
capital, the city was finally abandoned and the capital moved to .
meantime the population pursued its own meandering way, buil.
churches, and consumed a great deal more liquor in an attempt to en
disease other than cirrhosis should gain any ascendancy over them.

Where now the great churches stand in splendid isolation, they were c
surrounded by a maze of two-storeyed, red-tiled houses which filled the c   .d
spilled over into the villas and palaces of the suburbs. The houses extended along
the banks of the Mandovi as far as Raibandar, the ancient harbour of the Kings of
Vijayanagar, and sprawled south towards the old city of Gopakkapattana, now
called Goa Velha, so that most of the island seemed to be covered with villas and
houses, but the greatest concentration was in the city itself.

The wealthy suburb of Raibandar, with its imposing collection of magnificent
houses, was linked to Panjim by the Ponte de Linhares, built in the 1630s by the
Viceroy of the same name. This causeway is 3 kms long, and rests on a series of
arches which separate the bank on the Mandovi from the salt flats to the south, still
a major source of salt. The causeway was built by slave labour and currently
supports the road which links Old Goa with Panjim, however in former times the
majority of visitors to the city would have travelled by boat all the way.

Alighting at the pier of the Viceroys, the visitor would have been confronted by
one of the principal gates of the walled city. To the left was the main customs-
house, now totally destroyed, where recently discovered fragments of European
pottery, Portuguese tiles and Cambay-style earthenware, and a preponderance of
sherds of Wan-Li porcelain testify to the rich trade of the city. The street then passed
under the Arch of the Viceroys (pl. 12) through which these grandees entered the
city ceremoniously and which had been originally designed by Julio Simão.

12 The Arch of the Viceroys

celebrated engineer and architect, born in Goa to a family of Portuguese
...rs, had been sent back to Portugal to study. He eventually returned to Goa
where he became one of the principal architects, his greatest work being the
magnificent See Cathedral which he designed along with Ambrosio Argueiro and
where his remains are buried.

Crossing through the middle of the city was the Rua Direitta, the main street,
permanently thronged with merchants and customers of all kinds. Here was the
main gathering place and area both to see and be seen, while merchandise from all
parts of the world crammed the shops on either side and representatives of the
neighbouring potentates made purchases of horses and black slaves for their
masters.

Throughout this throng moved the robed figures of the priests. The image of the
church was omnipresent, and the ecclesiastical clangour of bells provided an
almost uninterrupted background to the tenor of daily life. Some fifty convents and
churches in the city bore witness to the manifest piety of the inhabitants, and the
encrusted wealth within them to the generosity and substance of the city at this
time. This piety however also had its negative side, and was maintained at a high
level of fervour by the kind offices of the Inquisition, whose officers and informants
seemed to be equally ubiquitous.

After the arrival of the Holy Office in Goa in 1560, the Viceroy presented them
with the old palace of Yusuf 'Adil Shah, having already transferred his own
lodgings to the fortress, and with the prospect of so many souls in mortal peril, they
commenced their activities with edifying zeal. The means used to save the souls of
the unnumbered accused who passed through these portals all too often destroyed
the rather more frail bodies which temporarily housed them. This however did not
seem to deter the Inquisitors, and every two or three years they crowned their efforts
with an auto-da-fé. At this impressive ceremony, which normally lasted two days,
one for the sentencing and one for the executions, the Church, in all its terrifying
majesty, allied with its Viceregal secular arm, confronted the heterogeneous
population with a spectacle of total unity, awe-inspiring in its complete
incomprehension of anything outside its own beliefs and traditions. Church and
State unanimous in their determination to crush any slight deviation from their
own strictly interpreted canons, and equally united in their intentions of imposing
these beliefs, by any means whatsoever, on an incomparably larger indigenous
population whose own ancient religious beliefs they made little or no attempt to
understand. Rarely has such total conviction been coupled with so complete a lack
of understanding that such actions might seem at variance with the creed preached
and could have the effect of turning people against that creed rather than causing
them to embrace it.

The Holy Office managed to keep Goa itself in a state of somewhat dogmatic
purity for the next two hundred years until it was finally abolished in 1774.
Fortunately for the administration its authority did not extend beyond the frontiers,
nor to the realm of foreign negotiations since at times the state only seemed to
survive by precariously balancing one alliance against another, none of them with
fellow Catholics. Equally fortunately the narrow standards of the Inquisition were
not universally held by all the clergy and in particular the Jesuits soon acquired and
developed the reputation for urbanity which has clung to them ever since. This was

particularly useful since they were employed on a number of occasions as ambassadors to various potentates, even if Shah 'Abbas of Persia did on one occasion ask that no more priests should be sent to him in a diplomatic capacity, 'because a religious out of his cell was like a fish out of water'.

While enthusiasm still welled among the population and the crusading zeal which had created the city in the first place had not really been blunted, the state was called upon to face one of its most severe attacks. Still flushed from the recent conquest of Vijayanagar, 'Ali 'Adil Shah of Bijapur determined that the time was ripe once again to attempt to reassert his sovereignty over Goa which the Portuguese had taken from his ancestors.

Had he managed to retain the alliance of all five Muslim kingdoms which had successfully destroyed the power of Vijayanagar it is possible that he might have been finally successful, but almost immediately after the fall of the Hindu empire, while the plunder was still being divided, dissensions had been apparent, and within months the kingdoms were once again warring with each other. However, in 1570 he did manage to form an alliance with the ruler of Ahmednagar to the north whose territory contained the port of Chaul where the Portuguese had another fort, and also the ruler of Calicut who was in a similar situation. The allies attacked on all fronts.

Calicut fell to the Muslim alliance, but the Portuguese repelled the Ahmednagar army at Chaul, and held that of Bijapur at Goa itself. The 'Adil Shah had an overwhelming superiority in manpower which he deployed on the landward side, surrounding the city with a wall of men and elephants, while the combined fleets managed to blockade the harbour to ensure that no supplies reached the defenders. Against this massive armament the Portuguese were only able to raise a few hundred soldiers coupled with some priests who were not unwilling to bear arms, and a small army of slaves who realised that their own welfare was coupled with that of their masters.

Attacked on all sides the great advantage of the Portuguese was their short lines of communication, but the main defense of the city lay in the swampy morass which surrounded it. Within this damp and sticky atmosphere, the total lack of hygiene took its toll, and after a siege which lasted nearly a year, the 'Adil Shah eventually withdrew his troops and the city was saved. The city itself suffered its own inevitable cholera epidemic in sympathy with the invaders, but it had survived a major attack from the Muslim forces and emerged even stronger as a result.

Within a very short time the city had more than made up for any loss in population. People flocked to it from all sides and it enjoyed a prosperity unrivalled in the world. Other cities might be equally as large, although at this time there were precious few, but no others enjoyed so many additional advantages. Outside the city itself the climate and the atmosphere were perfect, and in the rich villas which spread over the whole area the upper classes led a magnificent life of unparalleled ostentation and debauchery. At all levels of society, as far as means would permit, a similar life, if perhaps in a less exaggerated form, was the chief aim.

A number of travellers have left us vivid descriptions of life in Golden Goa, many of whom, such as Albert de Mandelso who visited Goa in 1639, were regally entertained by the Viceroy with all possible splendour and whose descriptions reflect the magnificent life of the rulers. Fortunately we also have the descriptions of others to counteract the favourable impressions received by the rich and famous, and which enable us to peek under the skirts of this apparently elegant lady and see the vice and squalor upon which this genteel facade was based.

In 1608 François Pyrard visited Goa and his account is a very useful counterbalance to the usual impressions received by other writers. Despite the efforts of the Inquisition morals were extremely loose in Golden Goa, and many women were apparently eager to sleep with and indeed live with Europeans to such an extent that they were prepared to keep them in return. Children of such a union, even though of unwed parents, were able to inherit from both parents, which was also apparently an added inducement. Pyrard's description of the idle life lived by these Europeans, supported by their women, makes extremely amusing, if at times somewhat scandalous, reading.

Handsome soldiers were also in great demand among the higher-class women, and apparently the wives used a potion made from the Datura plant which had the ability of rendering their husbands insensible; the wives were then able to admit to the house whomsoever they wanted without the husbands being aware of it. The exact formula of the Datura potion had to be carefully worked out since it is also a lethal poison, but apparently small doses merely rendered the recipient insensible.

By the seventeenth century life in Goa was completely decadent, and the whole economy was dependent on slaves. Slaves would in fact totally support their owner, either by indulging in retail trade, so that the majority of the shops were actually managed by slaves, or by direct prostitution. Pyrard's description of the Goan facts of life lacks nothing in detail and all sections and classes provide equal opportunities for his pen.

One of the earliest and certainly the most distinguished writer who visited Goa was the great Portuguese poet Luis Vaz de Camões, known in English as Camoens. After a brief military sojourn in North Africa at Ceuta where he lost an eye, presumably in a battle, he left for India in 1553. He had arrived in India after what he described as six months of very unpleasant life at sea, and had to embark again almost immediately to make war against the ruler of Malabar. He subsequently took part in an expedition to the Straits of Mecca, and even found himself involved in a voyage to China together with a shipwreck at the mouth of the Mekong river. Before he left in 1570 he had served under eight Governors or Viceroys, was just as poor as when he left Lisbon, but had written his great poem *Os Lusiadas*, the national epic of the Portuguese.

After his long and dreadful journey which cost the lives of many of his compatriots, his first impressions of India were favourable, but he also described India as an indulgent mother to the unworthy and a cruel stepmother to the worthy, a penetrating criticism which time must have deepened.

Although written in the Orient *The Lusiad* has almost no descriptive passages about Goa, as the *Aeneid*, to which Camoens owes a great debt, has no description of Rome, but from its pages we can obtain a brilliantly conveyed impression of the way in which the Portuguese of that period thought, and the inquisitive driving force which enabled them to create such an empire. For a superb series of pictorial representations of the Portuguese at the same period however, we must turn to the famous Japanese nanban byobu, 'the southern barbarian screens'.

After the first contact in 1543 when three Portuguese trading ships were blown off course and landed in Japan, so commercially important did the trade become that the Japanese found it necessary to establish a special port – Nagasaki – to handle the flow of foreign goods. As a result of this for a short period, 1590 to 1614, Japan went through a craze for Western things, and Western clothes became so popular among the nobility that the tailors in Nagasaki were kept busy day and night to meet the demand.

Coupled with this craze a number of superb screens were painted which showed the foreigners in great detail, their ships, their clothes, the parasols carried over them, their priests, and also the merchandise they brought. Although a number of Japanese had taken advantage of the Portuguese ships and had travelled to Europe to see these strange ways for themselves, and some paintings produced by Japanese artists at this time owed much to European techniques, the nanban screens were produced in a purely traditional way. Pigments were applied in the same way they had been for centuries, the backgrounds were still done in gold leaf, and little or no attempt was made to portray perspective so that conventional golden clouds continued to divide one plane from another.

The nanban screens were usually made in pairs, the left-hand screen depicting the arrival of the Portuguese ship in Nagasaki, while the right-hand screen featured the procession of the Captain-Major and his entourage through the streets. All of this is painted in great detail, with a certain minimal exaggeration forgivable when depicting such outlandish people, but nonetheless everything is recognizable and gives an extremely accurate idea of what such an arrival must have looked like. A change of background and an intensification of the numbers involved, plus unfortunately a loss of the fastidious cleanliness of the Japanese, gives a good idea of the bustle and the vivid colours which would have been the everyday scene in Goa at this time.

Apart from a wildly ostentatious display of clothes and other finery, all protected from the elements by rich parasols held by gaily dressed negro slaves, the other great love of the Portuguese in Goa was a rich variety of food and drink. The staple diet of the people was rice and fish, of both of which there was a plentiful supply, but for the rich this was augmented with beef, pork and poultry, as well as delicious varieties of shellfish with which the waters of Goa still abound. All of these were cooked in rich spices and washed down with quantities of imported Portuguese wines or with the local drink, feni, made from fermented palm toddy, and still the main drink of the Goans.

All of this however did not make for either empire builders or empire maintainers, and when the other European nations eventually arrived in India the once hardy Portuguese were in no real shape to put up much resistance, and while Golden Goa dreamed and played the empire slipped away from her fingers. Although the English were involved quite early on in this battle, it was the Dutch who were the principle attackers and the ones who gained most from the debris of the Portuguese empire.

The union of the two crowns of Spain and Portugal in 1580 was the initial reason for the major offensive which the Dutch launched against the Portuguese overseas dominions, although undoubtedly both England and the Dutch would have become embroiled with both of the Iberian powers eventually as their own commercial empires expanded. Certainly Philip II's efforts to suppress the revolt in the Netherlands, and his sporadic embargoes on Dutch trade with the Iberian peninsula and empires forced the pace of the attack, but an eventual confrontation between them was inevitable.

Neither the Dutch nor the English had any intention of accepting the Papal division of the world between Spain and Portugal, the situation for the growing northern commercial empires was an intolerable one. There was also the religious question to be considered. To the two Protestant nations, the Church of Rome was 'the Great Whore of Babylon' and the Pope himself a veritable anti-Christ, while to the Portuguese and the Spanish, both in the spiritual grip of the Inquisition, all Protestants deserved to be burned as heretics, and their appearance in eastern waters was in defiance of a God-given right which not only confirmed the lands themselves to the Iberians, but had also entrusted the salvation of the souls of the peoples of those lands to the hands of the true and indivisible Church. On both sides the war was regarded as just and holy, two seemingly inevitable concomitants to any major struggle.

The war was also to be world-wide, and the scale of the struggle waged by two small nations must excite admiration. Not only was the war waged in the cold latitudes around European waters, but all along the coast of Africa, the Indian Ocean, the islands of Indonesia and the Philippines, the estuary of the Amazon and the coast of Chile. Philip's empire encircled the globe, and the Dutch attacked it wherever it was possible, although as time went on it became more and more obvious that the only really successful attacks would be against the exposed sea-coastal Portuguese empire rather than against the great land-based Spanish vice-royalties of Mexico and Peru. In such a struggle Goa, the seat of the Viceroy and the greatest European city in the eastern world, was doomed to play a vitally important role.

The first attack by the Dutch came in 1603 when they blockaded Goa, but at that stage they were easily beaten off. By 1639 when they attacked again the result was much less predictable, and the eventual withdrawal was less the result of a successful Portuguese defence than of a long-standing ability to survive. By this time however the trade arteries which had pumped blood and money into the golden city for over a hundred years were slowly being severed or squeezed to such an extent that the life-force was failing to get through.

In 1605 the Dutch managed to capture the principal spice islands in the East Indies, and the Portuguese were forced to move to the south Celebes where they managed to maintain themselves in Macassar until 1667. Slowly the Dutch picked off the coastal settlements of the Portuguese empire until in 1641 they finally took Malacca. By 1658 they had also conquered the Portuguese settlements in coastal Ceylon, and in 1663 they captured Cochin and a number of other strongholds on the Malabar coast. Macao succeeded in holding out against attacks in 1622 and 1660, but soon it and Timor and a few other outer islands were all that was left of the Asian empire, even Hormuz having fallen to the Persians in 1622, with a certain amount of English help.

The Dutch were in fact once again blockading Goa in September 1641 when news arrived of the national revolution of December 1640 and the Portuguese independence from Spain. The Viceroy, the Count of Aveiras, hastened to proclaim

John IV as the king of Portugal and entered into immediate truce negotiations with the Dutch. Given the circumstances it is not surprising that they were in no hurry to accept them, and although the Dutch ambassador was received in Goa, negotiations dragged on for some considerable time. The Dutch governor of Batavia flatly refused to accept the truce and once again unsuccessfully blockaded Goa, although the official cause of hostilities had been removed by the separation of the two crowns.

The success of the Dutch in Asian waters was so swift and spectacular that it also alarmed the English and led to a complete reversal of alliances with an Anglo-Portuguese Truce which was signed in Goa in 1635. This alliance was to continue, in a fairly desultory fashion, and one of the earliest results was the marriage of Catherine of Braganza to Charles II in 1662 and the cession of Bombay and Tangier as part of the dowry. The peace which Portugal finally secured with Spain and the Netherlands in 1668–69, was also partly through English mediation and was perhaps a more tangible manifestation of English help.

However, there were certain fundamental problems which eventually were to lose the Portuguese the remnants of their precious supremacy. Although initially far superior to the native shipping, the Portuguese 'naus', with their four decks, were too large and heavy in comparison with the much lighter English and Dutch ships, while they were almost invariably weighted down with an excess of cargo which did little to enhance their manoeuvrability. The official trade monopoly was also maintained at all costs and, although private navigation was not prohibited, everyone engaged in it needed a license, which tended to ensure that all decisions were so long drawn out and complicated they stifled any initiative.

In an attempt to police their seas the Portuguese also needed many ships. In 1631 there were 115 ships in service and the shipyards of Chaul and Bassein were required to build a galleon every year, while this would have been supplemented by a yearly fleet from Portugal. Such a navy was required not only against the various enemies from Europe but also against the so-called 'pepper ships'. These were privateers engaged in pepper smuggling, buying it in South India and selling it wherever possible. As long as these were merely privateers the Portuguese could almost cope with the problem but when it was taken up officially by the Dutch and English East India Companies the whole edifice of monopolistic protection collapsed.

Money was almost always short so that payment of salaries and subsidies was generally in arrears, no matter what the rank of the persons involved. Subsidies were even sometimes diverted, funds previously allocated for the support of seminaries being switched to defence purposes, and in March 1626 it was ordered that no new monasteries should be constructed, while the subsidy for the ruler of Cochin, known as the 'copas de el-rei', was frequently late necessitating a letter to the king of Portugal from his 'brother'.

The close control which the Court in Lisbon attempted to exercise over Goa and which had such stultifying results, was exemplified in the series of administrative inquiries of all sorts. This general current of suspicion spared no-one, even the governors or viceroys themselves were often subjected to such inquiries once their term of office was completed, and these often lasted for several years, even after the death of the person concerned, when his family had to bear all the consequences.

With such a potential Sword of Damocles over their heads it is surprising that any pertinent decisions were ever made at all.

In the rest of the empire Portugal was somewhat more successful against the Dutch, managing to hold on to her East African possessions, but losing the chain of Gold Coast castles which had been the first foundation of the empire. In Brazil the Dutch eventually failed completely and the sugar trade of Brazil was finally left in the undisputed possession of the Portuguese. All of this however was of little help to Goa, and the great city, once the centre of a majestic empire, was slowly reduced to the status of a coastal town, more concerned with the intricacies of Indian diplomacy than with imperial administration.

This contrast between the old and new situations was naturally noticed and remarked upon by the new generation of travellers. John Fryer, an Englishman who visited the city in 1675, noted that the city still presented a noble appearance, and the inhabitants still made an attempt at display despite their increasing misery, but it was the 'splendid outside' which he noted, which had no real substance behind it. The administration was in a ruinous condition, and the river was silted up to such an extent that it was difficult to put into Goa itself. At this point a number of events which had been taking place in India suddenly assumed considerable importance for the very existence of Goa and the city was once again caught up in the maelstrom of Indian politics.

THE STATE OF INDIA

In the sixteenth century the Great Mughal, Akbar, was too wise to meddle seriously in Deccani politics. As long as his realm was safe from invasion from the south he was content to accept homage from the Deccani rulers and to leave them alone to pursue their internecine squabbles, while he was able to debate theology with various learned divines, including a number of Jesuits from Goa. This policy was to continue under his immediate successors until Aurangzeb, having governed the Deccan for his father Shah Jahan, seized the throne in 1659.

Fratricidal wars and the re-ordering of the Delhi administration diverted his mind from the Deccan for a while, but in 1681 he began the long series of campaigns in the south which only ended with his own death twenty-six years later. During this time he finally ended the rule of the 'Adil Shahis of Bijapur as well as the Qutb Shahis of Golconda, and was not unnaturally the subject as well as the occasional object of much official correspondence from Goa.

During this same period another group appeared in the south which was also to have very considerable influence on Goa, the Marathas. This people lived along the Western Ghats, spilling over into the narrow coastal plain of the Konkan and also across the Deccan towards central India. Hindu by religion, they were welded together by their great leader Sivaji in the mid-seventeenth century, and by the time of his death in 1680 he was the ruler of a compact and well-organized kingdom in western India. Initially the Marathas were too insignificant to attract the attention of the Mughals, but after a personal encounter between Aurangzeb and Sivaji had ended in failure because of mutual suspicions, the Emperor was to spend the last years of his life fighting his descendants.

Sivaji seems to have been first noted in the official Goan correspondence as early as 1658 when he first started to carve a territory out for himself from the kingdom of Bijapur, of which his father was a vassal. At this time he was apparently favoured by Aurangzeb as a counter-balance to the 'Adil Shah, and his increase of territory favourably viewed. The fact that this territory marched alongside the northern Portuguese lands around Bassein and Chaul was however of considerable interest to the Goans, and an official correspondence was soon inaugurated with Sivaji as with the other neighbouring rulers.

In 1664 Sivaji plundered the rich Mughal port of Surat and directly incurred Aurangzeb's wrath, after which things began to become more complicated for the Portuguese. Aurangzeb sent letters to them demanding assistance against the Marathas, while Sivaji, a much nearer neighbour, also required help. The subsequent tone of the various Vice-regal letters is an object lesson in diplomacy, and despite a number of incursions into Goan territory in pursuit of rebel landowners, was successful in keeping the Marathas out of Goa, and both they and the Mughals remained in diplomatic contact with the Portuguese.

After the death of Sivaji in 1680 the Portuguese made haste to acknowledge his son Sambhaji as his successor, but equally when in 1683 the Viceroy learned of the approach of a Mughal army, he gave orders to the Captain General of the north to allow that army a liberal passage through Portuguese jurisdiction in order to avoid a conflict with the powerful Mughal emperor. In retaliation for this Sambhaji captured some Portuguese ships and set fire to some villages in the north, but he must also have decided about this time to destroy the Portuguese dominion entirely as a potential source of danger to his kingdom.

In 1683 Sambhaji laid siege to Chaul with a large army, and the city only just managed to hold out against him. One of the main problems of the defenders appears to have been that for some indefinable reason the care of the ammunition and other accessories of war had been given to the Church fathers, and no one could in consequence fire a cannon without their permission. Since practice however desultory requires the expenditure of gunpowder, etc., and therefore expense, none had taken place in some cases for fifteen years, and the cannon-carriages gave way at the first shot. And then there was no more ammunition at all!

With Chaul in such straits the Viceroy made a diversionary sortie to attack Ponda, then within the territories of Sambhaji, but this ended in total disaster with a precipitate retreat back to Goan territory. The effect however was even more disastrous in that it had brought Sambhaji in person to the region of Goa itself and he then launched an attack upon the home territory.

A sortie was sufficient to capture the fort of Santo Estevao from the sleeping soldiery, and the Viceroy was almost killed in attempting its recapture and forced to flee back to the city with the remnants of his soldiers. This was followed by an attack on the provinces of Bardez and Salcete and it seemed as though nothing could save the stricken city, already a shadow of its former glory, with an enfeebled population decimated by disease. In these circumstances the Viceroy turned to supernatural aid.

Having proved himself as a soldier the Viceroy had recourse to the protection of St Francis Xavier, and after prayers and litanies in honour of the saint, the tomb was opened. The Viceroy then placed in the tomb his baton, royal credentials, and a personal letter in which he gave the saint the charge of the state in the name of the most serene king of Portugal, and then prayed at the head of the saint having done all he could both as statesman and Christian.

Fortunately for Goa at this moment the Mughal army under the command of Shah 'Alam, son of Aurangzeb, approached, and Sambhaji was forced to withdraw and meet this major threat, and was occupied in fighting the Mughals until his death a few years later in 1689. What the Portuguese themselves had been unable to achieve through the sword, had apparently been achieved through the miraculous intervention of St Francis. The city went mad with Te Deums and the church bell threatened to destroy what was left of the buildings.

By this time Golden Goa was a relic – only the administration and the clergy still remained in crumbling mansions surrounded by the glorious churches and basilicas which still soared out of the ruins. Most of the rest of the people had either left or been killed by the periodic epidemics which continued to sweep the city. A number of factors contributed to this sorry state of affairs, but certainly chief among them was the insalubrious condition of the site, and the consequent loss of life.

Already in 1582 the municipal council writing to the crown alleged that the city had become noticeably unhealthy after the great siege of 1570–1, and the position steadily deteriorated over the next two centuries. The porous nature of the soil which allowed drainage to seep into the wells from which the population drew its drinking water, and the increased incidence of malaria from the mosquitoes were the two main reasons for this high mortality. To be brought into the city was to court disaster, and the records of the Royal Hospital for Soldiers at Goa showed that 25,000 men died there in the first thirty years of the seventeenth century, not counting those who died in their billets, or when serving on board the fleets. Those citizens who were restricted to the city were not much better off, and whole areas became depopulated and were left in ruins.

Under the circumstances it is hardly surprising that a decision was made to leave Goa and to transfer the capital to a healthier part of the territory. The Conde de Alvor was still the Viceroy, the same who had placed the city in the care of St Francis, but he realised that the saint could do little to restore the city to its former glory, and decided to move to the southern peninsula of Marmagao. After much debate and soul-searching work was eventually started on the foundations of a new capital, but progress was of necessity very slow since the treasury was empty, and even the destruction of old buildings in Goa to provide materials for new ones in Marmagao took time and therefore money.

The continual changes of viceroys during this period did little to ensure any continuity in policy, although the Conde de Alver, upon his return to Lisbon, did have considerable influence at court and was therefore able to push the Marmagao idea. His removal from power in 1707 was the signal for total inertia to resume control, and the entire Marmagoa project was quietly buried, along with a great part of Goa itself. The attempts to move the capital, even though unsuccessful, had been calamitous for the old city. Buildings had been torn down for their materials, and no houses had been repaired in expectation of the removal. The result was total collapse and decay, at least in comparison to the great days of the sixteenth century.

This picture of decay must not however be taken as applying in such totality to the whole territory. Goa was still the centre of a considerable trading empire, and even while fighting the Marathas had been able to send fleets to the aid of Mombassa when that African colony was being attacked by the Omanis, the other great enemy of the Portuguese empire during his period. The end result may not have been so successful, Mombassa was lost in 1698, and the Omanis managed to capture many of the Portuguese coastal stations in the succeeding years, but it is some measure of the health of the supposed invalid that Goa was able to fight on two such diverse fronts at the same time, and at least give a good account of herself.

In addition, although many of the spices of the East Indies no longer came to Goa because of her European competitors, the gold and ivory of East Africa continued to do so, at least until the middle of the eighteenth century. Goa was also an important centre of the diamond trade until 1730, more so perhaps than Madras, the newly founded English city on the east coast of India, and the East Indiamen which sailed from Goa to Lisbon were still richly laden, even if there were only one or two a year instead of five or six. By the middle of the eighteenth century the economic capital of the Portuguese empire had certainly shifted to Brazil, but Goa was still of immense importance, even though the city itself had suffered cruelly and was apparently in an advanced state of decay as far as the citizenry was concerned. Surprisingly enough however, even at this time, many of the great churches and convents were still being rebuilt and adorned; the Church at least was still a powerful force.

From the suburb of Panelim, where the Viceroy had shifted his residence in 1695, the administration continued, and it was to that place that in 1737 came the news that the Marathas had struck again. After the death of Aurangzeb in 1707, Shapu, the son of Sambhaji, had been released from prison and had returned to regain his kingdom. As soon as he was firmly established on the throne of his father he began operations against the Portuguese, at first merely minor assaults, but with his sights firmly set on the Province of the North and its capital Bassein.

The Province of the North was the richest and most productive part of what Indian territory remained to the Portuguese after their disastrous wars with the Dutch and the Omanis, It comprised the Portuguese settlements along the sixty-mile stretch of coast between Bombay and Daman to the north, and in some areas extended twenty or thirty miles inland. The ruins of Bassein still testify to its former wealth, and indeed the estates of most of the nobility and clergy of Goa itself were also situated in the Province of the North, so that its eventual loss was a devastating blow.

This Luso-Maratha war lasted for two years, from early 1737 until peace was finally concluded in May 1739, and was a war of attrition in which the Portuguese defenders showed themselves worthy of their great heritage, and earned themselves such praise that from then on any brave fighters gained from the Marathas the title 'Warriors like the Portuguese'.

After capturing a number of fortresses in the north, the Marathas employed diversionary tactics and sent a major force against Goa itself at the beginning of 1739. This was initially successful, and effectively prevented any further help being sent to Bassein from the capital. Margao was captured and Rachol besieged, and the nuns and priests, together with various sacred relics and treasure were evacuated from Goa to the fortress of Marmagao. Bardez and Salcete were overrun, and had the Marathas realised how desperate were the conditions in Goa, there was little that could have resisted their complete capture of the entire Portuguese territory.

Fortunately for the Portuguese, the defence of Bassein and some of the northern fortresses so impressed the Marathas that they agreed to peace talks, which were finally signed in May 1739. Goa lost the entire Province of the North with the exception of the port of Daman, and in return for the withdrawal of the Maratha forces from the remaining Goan territory, agreed to pay a huge war indemnity, which effectively crippled the state and the population. The whole affair was a total disaster and although relieved by individual acts of courage and bravery, the attack demonstrated the complete disorder into which the state had been allowed to fall, and at the same time the immense power of the priesthood which had been able to countermand decrees of the Viceroy even at this time of crisis. The end of that system at least was at hand.

Already Prime Minister, the Marquis de Pombal found his power in Portugal consolidated as a result of the great Lisbon earthquake which laid over two-thirds of the city in ruins. This resulted in the King turning to Pombal to guide him through the ensuing crisis, a position which he was to hold for the next twenty-two years until the King's death. During this period a number of sweeping reforms were made, mainly concerned with development of Brazil, by this time the most important remaining part of the Portuguese empire, but a number of them had equally important effects on Goa.

The first most important decree was the confiscation of all Jesuit properties throughout the Portuguese world, and the imprisonment or deportation of the members of the Society. Although this did not yield the treasure in gold and diamonds which was supposed to have been hidden within their houses, it did bring considerable quantities of land to the Crown, and effectively subordinated the religious to the royal ministers.

In the same way when the Inquisition was either abolished, as in Goa, or made use of, as in Portugal, it was always to increase the power of the Crown. At one time it was suggested that he was trying to follow the ideas of Henry VIII when he made the break with Rome in 1760, but Pombal was a staunch Roman Catholic, and was only too pleased when the Pope made sufficiently strong overtures in 1770 to heal the breach. None of these measures were directed against the Church as such, they were merely against the power that it had accrued over the centuries and which Pombal saw as encroaching on the Royal prerogative. If he was guilty of anything on this side it was of excessive 'regalism', the need to curb all other authorities and to make them subordinate to the Crown.

As regards specifically Goan measures, Pombal also became involved in the story of Goa, and gave most detailed and stringent instructions for its rebuilding. Legislating in far away Lisbon he was unaware of the real reasons for the various decisions to abandon the city, and saw only the loss of the once great capital of the Indies. This again touched his attitude towards the Crown in that he saw the loss as a diminution of the glory that attached to the king, and hence his stern and detailed edicts which required the various districts to give money and labour for the re-erection of the houses of the city. After his fall from power all work once again ceased and the city was eventually allowed to crumble away peacefully when the capital was officially moved downstream to Panjim.

One other measure of Pombal's, however, was in the most enlightened European tradition, and this was fortunately continued after his fall. Although not legally sanctioned there had long been an unofficial colour bar exercised against Indian Christians in the Portuguese territories. A number of appeals had been made against this practice, and Rome was convinced that the formation of a native clergy was essential for the sound development of Christianity in Asia. The difficulty was in putting such ideas into effect against the inherent prejudices of both lay and clergy on the spot.

Rome had been aware of this problem since the mid-seventeenth century, but it was not until Pombal was in power that anything actually happened. In 1761 he promulgated a decree which informed the Viceroy and the Governor-General of Mozambique, that henceforth the Asian and East African subjects of the Portuguese Crown who were baptised Christians must be given the same legal and social status as white persons who were born in Portugal, since 'His Majesty does not distinguish between his vassals by their colour but by their merits'.

This decree was followed by a further one in 1763 but to no avail, and it was only when the Indian secular clergy sent a petition directly to Pombal that anything serious happened. In 1774 not only did he despatch a new Viceroy to Goa, but also a new Archbishop, with strict instructions not only to enforce the anti-racialist legislation which had been quietly shelved by their predecessors, but actually to favour the claims of the Indian clergy above those of their European confreres. This was eighteenth century enlightenment at its best, and fortunately the government of his successors was wise enough to continue the policy.

This policy became so much an integral part of the Portuguese administration that when in 1787 there was a plot to overthrow the Portuguese and establish a republic in Goa, a plot which was organised by some of the native clergy who had gone to France, there was no subsequent change in the policy towards the native clergy. The plot itself was discovered at a very early stage and was ruthlessly suppressed, but the anti-racialist policy continued. By the time of the suppression of all religious orders throughout the Portuguese empire in 1834–5, out of some 300 regular clergy in Goa, only 16 were Europeans the rest being Indians. Pombal's anti-racialist policies were not so successful in East Africa, but in India they represented a major break-through which was much in advance of happenings in the rest of Asia.

Meanwhile the Goans had in no way totally accepted the loss of the Province of the North, and throughout the eighteenth century attempts were made to regain it. Not only however did the Marathas prove too strong, despite a number of internecine feuds, but the British were also increasing in power and expanding from the base which the Portuguese had given them on the west coast – Bombay. In 1774 the British captured some forts in the former Province of the North contiguous to Bombay, and in 1780 they captured Bassein itself, despite numerous strong protests from the Portuguese. Eventually in 1783 and 1785 the Portuguese did manage to reclaim part of the province in the area around Daman which, together with the port of Diu in Gujarat, they were able to retain.

Partly in compensation for the loss of the Province of the North a number of moves were made to enlarge the Portuguese holding in the area directly around Goa, and it was at this time that the so-called New Conquests were acquired. In 1781 Bicholim was conquered, followed by Satari in 1782, while Pernem was ceded in 1788. Finally by the treaty of 1791 the King of Sunda ceded Ponda and the rights he had to Sanguem, Quepem, and Canacona, as well as the island of 'Cabo de Rama' which had already been captured in 1763. Goa thus assumed its present dimensions and constituted a much more compact territory than previously.

Goa was unable to escape involvement in the Napoleonic wars, and in 1798 the Marquis of Wellesley decided that it was necessary to defend Goa against both the French and their ally Tippu Sultan, ruler of Mysore. A fleet was sent to Goa but was politely rejected by the Portuguese Viceroy and left, but returned in 1799 and, despite local protests, disembarked British troops near the Fort of Aguada, where they encamped for a while before once again withdrawing. In 1802 they returned and this time Goa was in fact under British occupation, and although most of the troops were removed by 1810 as a result of Portuguese protests, the rest only left in 1813.

The beginning of the nineteenth century also saw the end of Maratha power. By 1818 and the conclusion of the third Anglo-Maratha war, this was totally eclipsed and the once proud rulers of almost half of India reduced to British pensioners.

British power was supreme, and as this slowly engulfed most of the country, the Portuguese territories gradually slipped into an indolent somnolence from which events were only very occasionally to rouse them.

In the meantime the capital had finally shifted from Goa to Panjim, and the nineteenth century saw the creation of a new capital, although not on quite as splendid lines as the old one. The process of moving was a gradual one, and as usual was led by the Viceroys in an attempt to find the most salubrious quarters. In 1695 they had already moved to a palace in Panelim, a suburb of Goa, but by the end of 1759 they had decided to move to the old palace of the 'Adil Shahs at Panjim. It had obviously been kept in a reasonable state of repair because it was here that the new Viceroys landed and spent the nights before their official entry into Goa. The palace was large, but was altered on a number of occasions, particularly in 1887 and later in 1900, but remained the residence of the Viceroy or Governor General until 1918, after which they moved to the Cabo Palace, formerly the convent of the Franciscans.

At the beginning of the nineteenth century Panjim consisted of the palace which towered over everything else, a few government buildings, and about 200 houses, which might be considered a somewhat inauspicious beginning for a new capital. In 1819 the High Court and the Accounts Office both transferred to Panjim, and then in 1821 the first of a peculiarly Goan institution appeared, the Gazeta de Goa, the first periodical in the Portuguese State of India. Since that time a considerable number of journals and newspapers have appeared, because Goans apparently like to rush into print, and the various causes of the nineteenth and twentieth centuries have all had their journalistic promoters and commentators as much in Goa as in the rest of the world.

Dom Manuel de Portugal e Castro, who was Viceroy from 1827 to 1835, is regarded as the 'Founder of the New City', and he erected many buildings and made spacious roads. He also created the esplanade along the Mandovi which had formerly been a series of sand dunes, built five primary schools and founded the Public Library. The Customs House was also built at this time, and Dom Manuel transferred the Mint to Panjim from Panelim, as well as building a number of military constructions to safeguard the city.

Slowly Panjim became a capital city, and more and more buildings were erected or improved to beautify it. One of the oldest buildings in Panjim which is at the centre of the city is the church of Our Lady of the Immaculate Conception (col. pls. 5–6). This church was originally founded at a very early stage in Goa's history, certainly before 1541, and was rebuilt from the foundations in 1619. Over the centuries it has been added to and adorned with new altars and chapels, and its double processional staircase, rising in a series of angled planes from the square, still forms the focal point of the city's religious feasts.

The first Senate in Asia was founded by Albuquerque in 1511 and occupied the Senate House in Old Goa between the Cathedral and the Palace of the Inquisition. In 1835 it was moved to Panjim, and after a series of peregrinations, eventually moved into its own building in 1869, unfortunately demolished in the twentieth century. The High Court building however, is still in use. Built in 1878 it is presently the Court of the Judicial Commissioner.

One of the more interesting churches in Panjim, which also contains a strong link with the territory's past, is the Chapel of St Sebastian in Fontainhas ward.

Although built in 1888 it is particularly noteworthy because it contains the crucifix which was originally used in the palace of the Inquisition in Old Goa. This crucifix was transferred to the chapel of the 'Adil Shah Palace in Panjim, and from there in 1918, when the palace was no longer used as the residence of Governor General, it was moved to its present site. The image is unusual in that the eyes are open and the head is held erect, presumably acting as a symbol of awareness which would have carried an important connotation in its original emplacement.

As the city grew so also did its political consciousness, and the move away from Portugal, either to found a republic, or as an integral part of the nationalist movement in India, slowly gathered momentum. This move was intimately linked with the liberal ideas current in Portugal, and when Portugal herself was torn between the absolutist supporters of Miguel and the liberals under Peter IV, it was reflected in the colonies. When the war between the two brothers ended in 1834 a constitutional charter was enforced under the child Queen Maria II, and as part of the subsequent reforms, the governorship of Goa was entrusted to a local man, Bernardo Peres da Silva, who was sent out to institute a programme of radical change.

Such a programme could only have been enforced with great difficulty under a senior Portuguese official, but under the direction of a local man who was inevitably seen as subject to factional pressures it was an impossible situation. A military revolt took place, and Dom Manuel de Portugal e Castro who was still in Goa was proclaimed Governor. He managed to send Bernardo Peres da Silva to Bombay, but was unable to prevent a series of revolutionary and counter-revolutionary moves involving the army which, not surprisingly, was also divided along with the rest of the population. This eventually culminated in the so-called 'massacre of Gaspar Dias', when the fort of Gaspar Dias was attacked by mutinous troops on 4 May, 1835, and the first regiment and the fort were utterly destroyed.

The government of Goa continued to reflect the dissensions in Portugal, but the governorship of the Conde de Torres Novas from 1855 to 1864 saw the inauguration of a great number of improvements. These did a certain amount to ameliorate many of the conditions against which the struggle was directed, but the movement, which had started with the plot by the republican-minded clergy in 1787, continued to grow despite suppression of various kinds.

Against this background there was still a certain involvement with local Indian problems, one of which was the appearance of the Ranes who had been forced south in the late eighteenth century. Originally a Rajput tribe, they spent the next hundred years either fighting the Portuguese directly, or being hired by them as mercenaries and then being forced to fight for arrears of pay. In 1895 one of these revolts necessitated the dispatch of an expeditionary force from Portugal. The Infante Don Afonso, Duke of Oporto and brother of King Carlos, accompanied the expedition and acted as Viceroy for a few months in 1896. While the expedition was attacking the Ranes in the northern part of the state he was able to use the Souza Gonçalves house in Guirim near Mapuça as his headquarters, an incident still recalled in Guirim.

Despite a certain degree of liberalisation during the nineteenth century there were still a number of major anomalies which continued and caused unnecessary offence and suffering. In 1905 a law was passed which effectively prevented

Hindus being teachers in primary schools, and although Church and State were officially separated after the declaration of the Republic in 1910, this was not so in the colonies, and a number of laws remained in force which had a purely religious bias. Many prominent Goans had drawn attention to these problems over the years and continued to do so both in print and in public and in public speeches. Francisco Luis Gomes, who represented Goa in the Portuguese Parliament of 1860, was a great economist and thinker who held the interests of all Goans close to his heart. He was able to call Europe's attention to the plight of Goa, but unfortunately he died in 1869.

It was however in the field of journalism that the Goan independence movement flourished, and a number of newspapers were produced, both in Goa itself and in neighbouring areas, particularly Bombay, which constantly made people aware of the continuing struggle. Naturally the papers which were produced within Goan territory had to compete with censorship problems, and were less able than their exiled colleagues to give free rein to their thoughts, but such journals as *O Heraldo*, *Nacionalista*, *O Comercio* and *O Debate* were important vehicles for many of the nationalist and independence ideas. Among the journalists who wrote for these papers Luis de Menezes Braganza must certainly be signalled as one of the outstanding figures of the early twentieth century in Goa, and the decision taken in 1963 on the twenty-fifth anniversary of his death to rename the Vasco da Gama Institute after him, was certainly an honour of which he would have approved. The palatial Menezes Braganza house in Chandor (see *col. pl. 33*, pls. 44–45) still retains many interesting mementoes of him, including his library, one of the largest private ones in Goa.

Prior to 1926 Portugal suffered a series of changing ministries as the new republic settled down, again reflected in her colonies. With the selection of Carmona as President, which post he held until his death in 1951, and the appointment of Salazar as Minister of Finance and later as Prime Minister, the Portuguese empire entered a new phase. Salazar effectively ruled Portugal for the next forty years, and his conservative and nationalistic views were clearly contained in the Colonial Act of 1930 which was to be the basis of Portugal's colonial empire until the end of the 50s. The subsequent changes which were introduced came too late to prevent the disintegration of that empire.

During the Second World War Portugal practised a form of neutrality compatible with the Anglo-Portuguese alliance, and the implementation of that policy in Goa allowed the Axis powers a neutral base in India which acted as a perfect observation post. It was however the end of British rule and the creation of an independent India in 1947 that was to signal the eventual end of the Portuguese empire in India.

Indian demands for the cession of Portuguese territories began in 1948, but were consistently rejected on the grounds that the territories were an 'integral part of Portugal'. In 1953 the Indian legation in Lisbon was closed, and in 1955 a mass invasion of Portuguese territories by *satyagrahis* (non-violent resisters) was repulsed with casualties. This led to the severance of all diplomatic contacts, although India still maintained her interest in a peaceful settlement. In 1961 there were a number of incidents along the frontier and tension increased to such an extent that on 11 December Nehru declared that 'India's patience is exhausted'.

Despite the insistence by many members of the United Nations on the necessity for negotiations, Indian forces entered Goa, Daman and Diu on 17 December, and the Portuguese formally surrendered on 19 December, thus ending a 450 year period of Goan history.

13 The Manueline carving on the doorway of the Church of St Francis of Assisi

THE CHURCHES OF OLD GOA

When the Abbé Cottineau de Kloguen visited Goa in 1827 he wrote: 'Nothing remains of the city but the sacred; the profane is entirely banished.' Apparently the churches and convents retained their grandeur but there was not a single decent house in the city; it was a vast solitude. In 1850 Richard Burton arrived in Goa, and the result of his journey was his first published work, *Goa, and the Blue Mountains: or, Six Months of Sick Leave*. The fact that he was on sick leave from his position as a lieutenant of the Bombay Army may have contributed to the somewhat jaundiced view of Goa which Burton took, but as usual his description of the various sites was masterly.

'Utter desolation' was his description of Old Goa, and the few people he did see only increased this sensation, 'as sepulchral looking as the spectacle around them'. He was comparatively unimpressed with the ruins, but again this may have been because of the difficulty of access, everything being covered with 'poisonous plants and thorny trees'. He also failed to appreciate the interiors, and compared them unfavourably to Italian village churches, but was awed at the size of some of the remaining buildings. Today the ease with which the remains can be approached and the landscaping which enables them to be seen and appreciated as well as the life which is slowly surging back around them would equally have appalled Burton, for he was nothing if not contrary, but this has created an opportunity to reassess the importance of these buildings. Now they can take their places as major monuments, both in terms of Christian architectural development, and also as important historical documents in the rich fabric of Indian architecture.

At the time of the conquest of Goa Portugal was enjoying the spectacularly prosperous reign of King Manuel I, 1495 to 1521, and during this period an outrageously rich architectural style was evolved which reached its highest point in the decoration of the churches in Batalha, Belem and Tomar. Much Portuguese decoration was inspired by Spain and France, but Manueline style decoration with its rich vocabulary of naturalistic motifs taken from sea creatures and tropical vegetation as well as nautical themes, ropes, anchors, chains, etc., has something completely non-Western about it. It is possible that the richness of these details relates more to the Hindu Indian architecture which the early arrivals found and examples of which they undoubtedly sent back in some form to Portugal. While such motifs as the cross and the armillary sphere are purely Western in concept, as are many of the other details involved, the manner in which they are presented, the exuberance of the decorative feeling, all of this has much closer parallels with the architecture of India than with that of Europe. Portugal, as the rest of the Iberian peninsula, had long been subject to Islamic influence, in architecture as in all other spheres of artistic expression, and the Mudejar style was a mixture, part Islamic part Gothic, which undoubtedly influenced Manueline styles as it did all other styles in the peninsula, but there is an extra outpouring in the Manueline style which is not Islamic. If this Indian connexion is real it is the first instance in Western history of direct influence on European art from beyond the European-Mediterranean world.

Unfortunately there is only one fragmentary remaining example of Manueline style architecture in Goa, and that is the doorway of the church of St Francis of Assisi (pl. 13). The Franciscans were the first missionaries to reach Goa after the reconquest, and in 1517 they obtained permission to erect a convent in the city. By 1521 the first buildings they owned were too small and therefore they built the Manueline church to which this doorway belonged. In 1661 it was showing signs of serious decay and consequently was pulled down and the present building erected incorporating the original doorway.

All of the churches in Old Goa are built either wholly or partly from local red laterite; basalt and the fine white limestone from Bassein, had to be imported and were used as decorative elements on the facade and to highlight particularly important architectural details on the interiors. The laterite exteriors were then covered in lime plaster to protect them from the weather, and this lime-wash had to be renewed after each monsoon, or at least fairly regularly, as a safeguard. Failure to maintain the buildings in this way meant that the heavy rains soon attacked the laterite and the buildings literally crumbled away.

Naturally, carved basalt details were expensive, and this probably helps to explain the re-use of the Franciscan doorway which sits so strangely on the classical facade, an exotic curvilinear form set against the squares and triangles of this late seventeenth century pastiche. The slender columns which become the mouldings of the trefoil arched doorway, are separated from each other by a band of carved flowers which have a squared outer shape. The somewhat small central lobe is surmounted by a moulded frame, crowned with a Greek cross and enclosing the royal Portuguese coat of arms and a superbly carved crown. This major armorial feature is flanked by two armillary spheres, and this whole upper section cuts right across the mouldings of the later facade, as if to say that the architect accepted the need to incorporate it into his design, but recognised its unsuitability and was determined to show that it had nothing to do with his classical building.

This fine doorway contains many of the best Manueline features, the curved arches, the armillary spheres, the rich carving and decorative quality, and the Greek cross, which was in fact the Cross of the Order of Christ, which Vasco da Gama and his fellow navigators bore on the sails of their ship; it does not however carry the twisted rope moulding which is always regarded as one of the hallmarks of the style. While this must have appeared in other parts of the original building, the honour of carrying it now belongs uniquely in Goa to the Church of Our Lady of the Rosary (*col. pl. 8*).

This church was built in 1543 on the Holy Mount and is a votive chapel built on the spot from which Albuquerque directed the battle between his forces and those of the 'Adil Shah at the time of the reconquest of Goa in 1510. The Chapel of St Catherine, the Church of St Francis and the Arch of the Viceroys were all originally built at an earlier date, but were each subsequently rebuilt, and the Church of Our Lady of the Rosary is therefore the oldest remaining church in Goa. It also has considerable claim to originality, its design reflecting a continuation of the

Manueline, Portuguese taste before everything was submerged in the wave of Italianate late Renaissance, early Baroque styles which swamped Goa with the arrival of the Jesuits.

The facade of the church consists of a large square three-storeyed tower portico, the main entrance being through its ground floor which acts as a porch. The west front of the portico is flanked by two engaged cylindrical towers whose cross-crowned cupolas rise to the middle of the second storey, while the side faces are flanked with two larger cylindrical towers rising to the third story, the southern of which contains a staircase giving access to the upper part of the church. The whole appearance of this portico, with its engaged cylindrical towers, gives an impression of solidity and strength, which is intensified by the use of the twisted rope moulding which literally ties the whole thing together. The rounded arches of the ground floor entrances add to this feeling of completeness, to which the carving of the rope mouldings adds just a touch of fantasy.

This concept of a tower portico facade is one which is found also in the church of Bassein as well as in the churches of southern Portugal from where it undoubtedly takes its origin, but it soon gave way to the more conventional facade, although towers continued to be an important feature in Goan churches.

The plan of the church is cruciform, the portico forming an extension of the nave, and with the windows near the roof, it gives the impression of a fortress. Although late Manueline in style, or at least partly so, the rib vaulting of the porch and the south transept have a Gothic influence, and in the interior, some of the decoration may be said to combine a certain Indian treatment, perhaps indicating the presence of native craftsmen at the time of construction. The tomb of Dona Catarina de Sa (pl. 14) alongside the High Altar certainly has considerable Indian influence, the lower panel and the engaged columns being purely Gujarat in style. Since it is extremely fine carving in marble it was very probably carved in Gujarat and imported to Goa via Diu, the Portuguese port there.

The first church built after the reconquest was the Chapel of St Catherine (pl. 15). This was erected by Albuquerque as an act of thanksgiving for his great victory over the Bijapuri forces in 1510, which had occurred on the 25 November, St Catherine's day. The first structure was of mud and straw, but a more solid one was built two years later, which was subsequently enlarged in 1530 or 1531 by means of public and private donations, and then raised to the status of a Cathedral by a Papal Bull of 1534. Until 1542 this Cathedral was the only parochial church in the city, and in 1557 it was made the archiepiscopal metropolitan church of India by a further Papal Bull, having apparently been rebuilt in 1550. In 1952, as part of a general restoration of the convents in the city it was largely rebuilt by the Portuguese government, so that only the form remains from the sixteenth century, but it has considerable historical interest.

Assuming that the facade is either original or a good restoration of the original, what is extremely interesting is that this modest Renaissance facade contains the germ of the most grandiose concept in Goa, the facade of the See Cathedral. The proportions are small and the strong line of the string course above the second storey tends to make the pediment and the tops of the two towers look like an afterthought, but the pediment is joined to the towers by scrollwork, and the towers themselves are an integral feature of the facade.

The See Cathedral (*col. pl. 11*) was begun in 1562, and was designed to be worthy of its position as the senior metropolitan cathedral for the whole of the Portuguese empire of the east. The money was raised from the sale of the property of any Hindus who died intestate and whose property therefore escheated to the Crown, and it was built on a site formerly occupied by a mosque. Other funds were also made over to it by the government, but work was still very slow and the main body of the church was not completed until 1619, and the altars not finished until 1652. The facade was probably completed in the 1620s.

14 The carved marble tomb of Dona Caterina de Sa in the Rosary church

15 The Chapel of St Catherine (courtesy Dept. of Information, Govt. of Goa, Daman & Diu)

The Cathedral was built for the Dominicans, but like so many other sixteenth and seventeenth century buildings in Goa, was strongly influenced by the work and designs of the Jesuits, particularly the Church of Il Gesu in Rome. This is one of the best known works of Vignola, the author of *The Five Orders of Architecture*, and in consequence was able to set the style for much subsequent building. In order to cope with the problem of a high central nave and lower side aisles, Vignola used the device which had been used originally by Alberti in the Church of S. Maria Novella, Florence, in the fifteenth century, whereby flanking scrolls connected aisles and nave into one composition. The Gesu was completed in 1584, some time after Vignola's death, and would therefore have been the most appropriate and up-to-date church to serve as a model for those in Goa.

The See Cathedral adopted this concept but in a considerably enlarged form, adding an entire storey to the Vignola design, and making one further significant modification which indicated the Portuguese rather than the Italian origin; the facade is flanked by two towers which actually extend the width. Flanking towers on the west facade of cathedrals were a common feature during the mediaeval period, but seem to have fallen out of favour during the Renaissance in most countries with the exception of Spain and Portugal. As already mentioned, the tower-facade concept was a feature of Manueline architecture, and towers were to continue as a feature of Goan architecture.

16 A detail from the life of St Catherine on the high altar of the See Cathedral

The towers are set back slightly from the line of the main facade, and perform an important function aesthetically in that they enlarge the width which compensates for the additional height of the extra storey. This also means that the interior plan of the cathedral is widened, introducing an aisle on each side between the nave and the side chapels. This gives the cathedral a much stronger cruciform shape than the Gesu, where the closely spaced chapels act in place of aisles.

In 1766 the northern tower was struck by lightning and collapsed so that the facade has a less imposing appearance than previously, although it now conforms to the more traditional concept of a single campanile. In fact the remaining tower houses a bell which is described as 'golden' from its rich sound which has been immortalized in poetry. The tower is plain for the lower two storeys but the upper two are ornamented with a pattern of pilasters, while the whole is crowned with an elegant balustrade.

These square towers may indicate a continuance of the Islamic minaret tradition which remained alive until the end of the fifteenth century in the Iberian peninsula. The square tower form was particularly strong in the western Islamic lands, and there are a number of examples remaining in Spain, the most famous being the Giralda of Seville.

The interior of the cathedral is of majestic proportions, the great barrel-vaulted nave, flanked by side aisles, and crossed by equally high transepts, forming an imposing sight (*col. pl. 12*), its whiteness providing a perfect foil for the great golden altar-piece which fills the entire west end. The aisles are approached through arched openings which rise to the springing of the barrel vault, and lead to a series of chapels which have a lower roof level and act as buttresses to support the weight of the roof. On the right hand, northern side, the Chapel of the Cross of

Miracles is particularly noteworthy, while on the other side the Chapel of the Blessed Sacrament (*col. pl. 13*) is so huge and beautifully decorated that it requires a major salient from the cathedral and even has its own vestry.

Like the earlier cathedral, the See Cathedral is dedicated to St Catherine of Alexandria, and the main altar-piece shows scenes from her life and martyrdom (pl. 16). This richly gilded wooden wall rises to the full height of the nave and is divided into sections by a series of columns and entablatures, each rectangular panel enclosing a semi-circular arch on pilasters which acts as a frame for the pictures. The whole effect is magnificent, the deeply carved panels catching the light from the side windows and shimmering in the sun.

Mention has already been made of the Manueline entrance to the Church of the Holy Spirit (see pl. 13), the Franciscan monastery church, the only remaining link to the 1521 building, and the only example of Manueline art in Asia. The rest of the facade is from the rebuilding of 1661 and is fairly undistinguished (pl. 17). There is only a single nave so that the same problem of disguising the transition from nave to aisles did not occur, nonetheless the pediment and scrolls are still retained as are the turrets, although these have now degenerated into purely decorative appendages, which are somewhat stunted and detract from the main lines of the facade. The whole upper storey has undergone a Baroque transformation from the classical severity of the Cathedral, a series of pinnacles adorning the broken pediment, between the two sections of which rises a granite cross. The central niche has a granite statue of St Michael in place of the St Catherine on the facade of the Cathedral.

After the somewhat unimpressive facade the interior of the church is a rich contrast, and is one of the noblest examples of Indian Baroque (*col. pl. 14*). The three doors lead directly into the nave under a broad gallery for the choir. Three chapels open off the nave on either side, followed by shallow transepts which maintain the cruciform shape. The altar-piece is another superb architectural creation in gilded wood which fills the east end behind the high altar. It is more architecturally conceived than the altar-piece of the Cathedral, and the lower section is actually pierced by an archway so that the tabernacle stands proud. The crucifix in the centre of the pediment is adored by a kneeling figure of St Francis, the founder of the Franciscans, along with the words Poverty, Humility and Obedience, the three vows made by the monks when joining the Order.

As in many Franciscan churches the interior was highly decorated, and although much has been obliterated, there is still much painting left particularly in the nave alongside the High altar where scenes from the life of St Francis are painted on wood. Many parts of the walls are ornamented with large painted flower patterns, and the finely coffered ceiling is heavily decorated with similar floral designs. Originally most of the interior surface area would have been painted and, with the immense quantity of gilding involved, the effect would have been overwhelming.

The adjoining convent also underwent considerable rebuilding, particularly during the eighteenth century. The cloisters were rebuilt in 1707, some of the dormitory cells in 1762, and new buildings were added in 1765. At present the convent houses the Archaeological Museum, with the sculpture galleries around the cloisters and a very fine Portrait Gallery on the first floor where some sixty paintings of the various Portuguese Governors have finally come to rest. As the Governors shifted their residences, so the paintings followed them around until they were moved eventually from the Secretariat to the Museum in 1962, and now provide a fascinating study in the evolution of court dress over the past four hundred and fifty years. Prior to the suppression of the Orders this church and convent were obviously well endowed and much frequented, and the silence in both is now all the more noticeable.

A much worse fate however befell the church and convent of the Augustinians, which at one time was the richest and most splendid in the city. Standing forlornly on top of the Holy Hill all that remains of these buildings is a section of one of the towers which originally flanked the church facade (pl. 18). Even in its present condition it is impressive, and is higher than any other building in the old city.

17 The facade of the Church of the Holy Spirit, the Franciscan monastery church

18 The ruined tower of the Augustinian church

The convent was first built when the Augustinians arrived in 1572, but speedily rebuilt in 1587 with a monetary grant from the Portuguese king. This building also proved to be too small, and by 1602 the church and convent had reached their final imposing form, a closely connected group of buildings occupying the highest point of the Holy Hill. When the Orders were suppressed in 1835 the buildings were abandoned, although the convent was used for some time by the Misericordia, a charitable institution. Eventually the main vault of the church collapsed, but the facade remained standing until 1931, looking impressive even as a ruin.

The Church, dedicated to Our Lady of Grace, was built with a single nave having a number of side chapels, so that the great towers actually flanked the church rather than forming an additional frontage as in the Cathedral. The same decorative scheme however was still used with the scrollwork linking the pediment to the two towers. Unlike the later Church of St Francis where the turrets have been so reduced that they detract from the design, the towers of the Church of St Augustine formed a perfect foil and created an even greater feeling of strength than achieved by the Cathedral facade.

The Augustinian church had the same orientation as the little chapel of St Anthony (*col. pl. 16*) which stands alongside it. This chapel is known as the Royal Chapel because St Anthony is the national saint of Portugal and is held in great veneration by the Portuguese. The statue of the saint contained therein was given the rank of a captain in the army and received the salary due to his rank, the statue actually being taken to the Treasury in solemn procession to receive the money.

The chapel was first built at the beginning of the seventeenth century under the care of the Augustinians and therefore also closed in 1835. It was however reopened in 1894 after being renovated, and in 1961 it was completely restored by the Portuguese government. The plan of this little chapel is most unusual in that the doorway, sited at the eastern end, is set in a semi-circular apse which serves as a vestibule, beyond which rises the actual facade consisting of the usual pediment and towers but in miniature. In its present restored condition it is extremely attractive, giving a good idea of how the remainder of the churches must have appeared, and forms a living centre for the monuments on the Holy Hill.

Nearby is the imposing Church and Convent of St Monica, one of the largest structures in Goa, although parts of it are now sadly ruined. Begun in 1607 it was not finished until 1627, and was the only convent for cloistered nuns in Goa at the time. The huge square building is three storeys high and is built around a sunken central courtyard known as the 'Vale de Lirio' which contains formal gardens and a small octagonal kiosk. The building has obviously suffered considerably over the years, possibly as a result of being built on the slope of the hill, and there are a number of buttresses supporting the structure both within the courtyard and on the exterior, while the original vaulting of the wide cloisters has been replaced by flat wooden ceilings.

19 Part of a painted ceiling from the Convent of St Monica

The church is within the southern part of the building and occupies a complete section between the facade and the cloister. It has a single nave leading to an imposing altar-piece, set in a deep, apse-like niche, and ornamented with figures of saints. Most of the original decoration has been lost beneath layers of white paint, but in the southwest corner of the main cloister there are the remains of some early wall paintings depicting people in seventeenth century costume (pl. 19). The convent was at one time exceedingly important and was known as the Royal Monastery on account of its patronage. At present it has been restored and is used by the Mater Dei Institute for Nuns which was founded in 1964 for theological studies for nuns of various congregations.

The only other building on the Holy Hill is the Church and Convent of St John of God which was built by members of that order in 1685. In 1835, like so many other buildings in Goa, it was abandoned by its builders, and in 1844 it was purchased by the nuns of St Monica's to be used as a residence for their chaplains and other employees. After being completely restored in 1961 by the Portuguese government it is now being used by a group of Franciscan nuns.

The church has the traditionally Goan facade of towers and pediment, but by this late stage the roles have been reversed and the pediment, surmounted by a large cross, rises above the level of the two towers. This concept had first occurred in the miniature facade of the Chapel of St Anthony, which faces it, and may well have inspired the architects who were equally faced with the majesty of the Augustinian church and might have tried this idea to at least express a difference from a church they could not hope to surpass.

Descending from the Holy Hill one is confronted with what is now undoubtedly the most important church in Goa, the Minor Basilica of Bom Jesus (col. pl. 18) which contains the imperishable body of St Francis Xavier, Conqueror of Souls and Saviour of Goa. When St Francis first arrived in Goa he went to live at the College of St Paul where he was one of the teaching staff, and after the death of the principal he took charge of the whole enterprise in the name of the Jesuits. As usual the church, which had been consecrated in 1543, proved too small and a larger one was built in 1560, by which time St Francis had died, and in 1554 his body had been brought back to Goa and placed in St Paul's, of which now nothing but a gateway remains, although in 1568 there were eighty-eight Jesuit Fathers providing instruction for over three thousand students.

By 1585 the Jesuits were so powerful that they needed to build their own professed house in the centre of the city, and by 1589 this was a reality and is now known as the Convent of Bom Jesus. This elegant structure, which had been built very quickly in spite of the opposition of the various other Orders, still however lacked a church. This was begun in 1594 and finally consecrated in 1605 as is recorded in an inscription, and in 1613 the body of St Francis was removed from the College of St Paul and placed in the Professed House, being moved to the Church in 1624 and to its present chapel in 1655. In 1964 the church was raised to the dignity of a Minor Basilica by Pope Pius XII, and is today the most venerated shrine in Goa.

The first thing which strikes the eye about the Church of Bom Jesus is that it is not white like all the other churches in Goa. It was originally lime plastered, with the exception of the main decorative elements on the facade which are of granite, but this was recently removed, and the red laterite of which all the churches in Goa are constructed, is nakedly revealed. The lime wash had a protective function and its removal may well have a deleterious effect on the construction, although in the meantime the aesthetic contrast with the other churches is very interesting. The Indian Archaeological Service is currently making efforts to have the lime plaster restored to its original condition as part of a programme of restoration and conservation which should extend the life of the building.

The facade is the richest in Goa, and at the same time, one of the least Goan in that there are no towers to act as supports to the central pediment. It was apparently modelled on the facade of the now destroyed church of St Paul which also had no flanking towers, both therefore more closely recalling the facade of the Gesu, the Mother Church of the Order in Rome. There is only one tower in the church and that is set most unusually at the east end on the south side of the apse. This single, displaced campanile gives the church a much more Italian flavour than any of the others, and this distinction is confirmed by the care which has been lavished on the decorative designs of the facade, the most beautiful architectural feature of the church.

While the facade retains the three classical orders of architecture which were such a feature of the Renaissance, the wealth of decoration, particularly the abundant use of scrollwork, place it quite firmly in the Baroque. The rectangular divisions of the facade are heavily accentuated by pilasters and deep string courses which cause strong shadows in the Indian sunshine, and within each of the panels thus created the form is further emphasized by another series of columns and pilasters, one on each side of the side panels and two framing each stage of the centre section.

As each storey diminishes in height so the decoration increases in complexity until the pediment is reached which, while undoubtedly having the most complex and ornate carving, reverses the scale and is larger than the preceding storey. Because it is so obviously the focal point, and because it is so richly carved, this does tend to give the facade a slight imbalance, an almost top-heavy feeling, which is disturbing. It is possible that this would be less noticeable if it were lime plastered and the contrast less striking, although the proportions would remain the same.

The carving has been carefully planned, each rising level prefiguring part of the theme of the succeeding one. The three circular windows, which are usually staggered so as to indicate the interior height of the nave and aisles as in the Cathedral, are at the same level because the church has a nave only, and the shallow pitched roof is totally concealed by the pediment and its side scrolls. The ornate strapwork surrounding these circular windows is a preparation for the intricacies of the centre panel of the pediment amid whose strapwork flying angels adore the name of Jesus (pl. 20). This is represented by the letters I.H.S., signifying Jesus in Greek, always an important feature on all Jesuit buildings, which are placed in the centre of a circle of winged angels' heads, the whole surmounted by a royal crown with a cross. The topmost pediment also contains a further adoring angel.

After the promise of the exterior the interior is less impressive. The modern wooden ceiling, with its intricately carved brackets which seem to look back to Hindu architecture for their inspiration, cannot compare with the great barrel-vault of the See Cathedral, but, as with the facade, it is the richness and intricacy of the

20 A detail from the facade of Bom Jesus

detailed ornamentation which is the chief glory of the church. The altar-piece is completely Baroque in style, twisted columns supporting flying angels, with the Trinity above and St Ignatius Loyola, founder of the Jesuits, in adoration below, the whole covered in pure gold which overlays a body of carving and chasing leaving not an inch clear. The same treatment is given the two flanking altars, the one dedicated to Our Lady of Hope, the other to St Michael, which thus provide a golden end to the nave.

The two transepts are exteriorised, giving the church a truly cruciform shape like that of Our Lady of the Rosary. The northern transept contains the Chapel of the Blessed Sacrament, while the southern has been enlarged to contain the Chapel of St Francis Xavier. Flanked by more twisted columns of gilded wood, the archway leading to the chapel is heavily gilded and partially closed by a gilded grille below which hangs a section of gilded wooden lattice to separate the chapel from the rest of the church.

The silver casket containing the saint's body (pl. 21) made by Goan craftsmen in 1636, rests on a high tiered plinth in the centre of the chapel, the whole rising to a height of six metres. The lowest tier is of red jasper decorated with carvings in white marble, while the middle section is of grey jasper ornamented with bronze plaques on each of the four sides representing four episodes in the life of the saint. Above this is a marble balustrade around which a series of white marble cherubs are carrying scrolls. The immense silver casket also has a number of scenes from the life of the saint chiselled in low relief, and was once studded with precious stones. The tomb was the gift of one of the last of the Medicis, Cosimo III, Grand Duke of Tuscany, and was the work of a Florentine sculptor, and finally assembled in position in 1698.

The body of the saint has suffered considerably over the years, various pieces having been removed at one time or other. Perhaps the most grisly story being that

21 The tomb of St Francis Xavier in the Minor Basilica of Bom Jesus

of the lady who was so overcome while praying at the feet of the saint that she bit off one of the toes. She then carried it away in her mouth and it is still kept as a precious relic in her family in Lisbon. In 1890 another of the toes fell off and is now kept in a crystal case in the Sacristy, but in the seventeenth century they were much more concerned about relics, and part of the arm was sent to Rome in 1615 where it is venerated in the Church of Gesu, and another part of the right hand was sent to Japan in 1619. The body has been exposed a number of times, the last exposition being in December 1974.

The Sacristy is linked to the Chapel by a corridor, and is particularly famous for its carved wooden doors set in a magnificent stone doorway. It contains a number of paintings as well as some beautifully carved chests and drawers with some of the church vestments. The vaulted ceiling is finely coffered, and it must have been originally a most impressive chamber. A small exhibition of objects associated with the church is now on display in an upstairs room which also gives a unique opportunity of looking down on the tomb of St Francis. The exhibition also contains a number of paintings of the life of the saint by a present day painter which are very interesting and appear to reflect a deep devotion.

Attached to the basilica by a beautifully arcaded courtyard and fronting onto the same forecourt is another vast monastery with a high, somewhat forbidding facade. This was formerly the Professed House of the Jesuits, completed in 1585 but only partially rebuilt after a fire in 1633. It now houses a few Jesuit fathers who maintain a modest teaching establishment in the best traditions of the Order.

The last major church remaining in Old Goa is one which is very different from all the others. This is the Church belonging to the Convent of St Cajetan (pl. 22), and was built by a group of Italian Theatine Fathers who reached Goa in the seventeenth century having been prevented from entering the kingdom of Golconda, their original destination. They applied directly to the King in Lisbon and were eventually given a Royal Letter in 1655 with permission to settle and the grant of land upon which the convent and church stand. The convent is still in use as a Pastoral College for newly ordained priests, and in consequence both it and the church are well maintained.

22 The facade of the Church of St Cajetan (Church of the Divine Providence)

Within the comparatively modest means of a Goan budget, not to mention the skills available, the Church of St Cajetan, or the Church of the Divine Providence as it is also called, is modelled on St Peter's in Rome. The facade has the giant Corinthian columns and pilasters invented by Michelangelo and incorporated into Maderna's final facade, but lacks the two side bays which extend the facade beyond the width of the church and link the portico to Bernini's colonnade. This was perhaps somewhat beyond the means of the Theatines, but they managed to achieve a most noble facade whose only concession to local taste was the two towers which crown the corners and which in elevation replace the small domes of St Peter's. It has been suggested that Maderna's original design had towers at the corners, and that these were finally demolished by Bernini, in which case St Cajetan's may well be a copy of Maderna's design for St Peter's, or at least a Goan translation.

An attempted regularisation of the facade has been made which is not altogether to the detriment of St Cajetan vis-à-vis St Peter's, and utilizes some other Michelangelo designs which were well known in Rome. The centre doorway is square, as in St Peter's, while the two rounded arched smaller doors, which in St Peter's flank the centre door, have been moved one section further out and replace the other square doors. Alternating with the three doors are four semi-circular arched niches containing statues of St Peter, St Paul, St John the Evangelist and St Matthew. Above the niches are semi-circular arched pediments, while over the round arched doors are triangular pediments, the alternating line being exactly that of the Palazzo Farnese and being repeated immediately above in the row of balustraded windows, as in the facade of St Peter's. This regularisation, and the use of circular windows instead of square panels, given the much smaller compass of the entire conception, appears to work in favour of St Cajetan's, although, as in Maderna's facade, the section above with the two towers has the effect of masking the dome and is therefore less successful. The ribbed dome is in the Roman tradition, although one would not suggest that it continues the competition. It rests on a drum which is pierced with semi-circular windows, and has a lantern with a domed cupola surmounted by a cross, and is a perfect foil for the facade.

The interior (*col. pl. 20*) continues this tradition, and is in the form of a Greek cross with a central dome. The nave and transepts have coffered barrel vaults, and are supported on piers with gigantic Corinthian pilasters, as in Rome. The church is particularly noted for its finely carved and gilded woodwork (pls. 23–24) which not only decorates the main altar, which is dedicated to Our Lady of Providence, but also the six other altars and the pulpit. The main altar is in the semi-circular apse and is free-standing unlike the other altar-pieces in Goa. This very deep apse, the only one with this shape in Goa, is flanked by two octagonal domed sacristies which align with the apse and enable the church to retain a rectangular exterior outline.

The centre of the church has a most unusual feature in that directly under the dome, covered with a square slab, is a well. There are a number of traditions regarding this well, which may have been dug by the architect either to drain the soil or to test the stability of the ground, but is very possibly the remains of the tank belonging to the Temple of Saptakoteshwara which was in this vicinity.

Rome was quintessentially the centre of the Baroque; its vaults, cupolas and arches had their origins in the architecture of the Roman empire, and the imperial

23 Detail of the rich wooden carvings on the pulpit and high altar of the Church of St Cajetan

24 Detail of the rich wooden carvings on the pulpit and high altar of the Church of St Cajetan

ideal found its continuation in the claims of the Papacy. This architecture was essentially earth-bound, rejoicing in the practical solidity of horizontal planes, consumed with concepts of majesty and wealth, and totally rejecting the dream-like, mystical aspirations of the Gothic. The Church of St Cajetan embodies this grandiose conception better than any other church in Goa, and is therefore perhaps more truly Baroque. In the other churches a much stronger Iberian and local tradition fused and grew out of a continuous development, whereas St Cajetan's is a magnificent single occurrence which had no descendants and founded no tradition. It is a truly Roman church set in Portuguese India, and apparently found no imitators.

The remains of a number of other churches still emerge like some ghostly visitation from the encroaching jungle, but for the most part they have joined the houses and palaces which served them and crumbled back into the soil under the combined influences of climate and vegetation. The Chapel of Our Lady of the Mount (*col. pls. 21–22*) still manages to hold back the jungle because of its exposed position on a hill to the east of the city, but its towerless facade looks somewhat mournfully across from the site which Albuquerque himself chose, and the great flight of steps leading up to it is woefully overgrown and crumbling.

One last monument is worthwhile noting in Old Goa, more from its historical associations than from its authenticity, and that is the Arch of the Viceroys (see pl. 12). This was entirely rebuilt in 1954 and again restored in 1971 so that nothing except the concept remains of the original. The statue of Vasco da Gama which surmounts it is also a replacement, although of more respectable antiquity, but the plaque which records the emplacement of the first statue in 1599 during the Viceroyalty of his great-grandson has been incorporated into the modern arch. The old arch also had a number of paintings recording Portuguese deeds in the East, but these were destroyed and the only other inscription remaining records the emancipation of Portugal from Spain in 1640.

So much for the extant remains of this once great city but in its heyday one of the most famous and important buildings was the immense Royal Hospital, of which no trace now remains. First built by Albuquerque in 1511, it was the first European hospital to be built in the East and, in its time, was one of the most remarkable institutions in Goa. It was completely rebuilt by the Jesuits in 1593 and was on a scale unequalled by any of its European contemporaries. At the beginning of the seventeenth century it housed as many as 1,500 patients but by the end of the century there had been a change of administration and treatment suffered accordingly. By the middle of the eighteenth century the building was a ruin and the hospital itself had been transferred to the former palace of the Viceroys in the suburb of Panelim, like the rest of the inhabitants, fleeing the insalubrious climate of the old city.

PORTUGUESE ARCHITECTURE OUTSIDE THE CAPITAL

While the greatest concentration of monuments was obviously in Old Goa and subsequently in Panjim, there was no lack of churches distributed throughout the territory, many of which are of considerable importance. Whether in towns, or villages, or even in the middle of the open countryside, the white, lime-plastered churches form an integral part of the Goan landscape, and their gleaming maintenance is a loving manifestation of the devotion they continue to arouse.

In Goa Velha, the old Gopakkapattana, Pilar Monastery (*col. pl. 23*) is an ancient institution founded in 1613 which is still flourishing as an important religious and educational centre for Christian Missionaries. A new building houses the present teaching establishment, but the old church is still maintained within the compound and is a fine example of Goan seventeenth century architecture and contains relics of a Goan saint, Fr. Agnelo d'Souza who died in 1927. The old monastery lies behind the church, its double-tiered cloister enclosing a square formal garden, and still forms the centre of the entire establishment.

The Convent was apparently sited on top of a hill which had originally been crowned with a temple of Shiva who was worshipped locally under the name Goveshwar. A number of relics of this temple have been unearthed, some of which can be seen in the Seminary, among which are a headless granite Nandi Bull, the vehicle of Shiva, and a Naga serpent carved on another block. A piece of stone lattice, similar to those in various Kadamba temples is actually built into part of the convent wall. In 1962 a small mud-walled cave was discovered within the grounds and a few Nagas and other deities were found cut in high relief on the walls, and these are also in the Seminary, while at the foot of the hill, in the Convent orchard are the remains of a water tank which would have served the temple.

Whether this siting of the convent was the result of a Portuguese destruction of the temple, or whether it was part of the earlier Muslim devastation is unknown, but the site of the great Seminary at Rachol is certainly on that of a former temple which was one of five destroyed by Diego Rodrigues in 1564. The fort at Rachol was of great importance during the Maratha wars, and the Seminary itself is also built like a fort, crowning the hill and commanding a sweeping view on all sides. The fort has now almost disappeared, but the Seminary still guards the river, although there are few trespassers these days.

The fort was one of the most ancient in Goa. Originally Muslim, it had been captured from the Idalcan by the ruler of Vijayanagar in 1520, who then ceded it to the Portuguese. At one stage it had as many as 100 guns, but these were removed after the Maratha threat was withdrawn and by the mid-nineteenth century the fort was allowed to disintegrate.

By contrast the Seminary, transferred to Rachol from Margao in 1580, has enjoyed a continuous history as one of the leading educational centres in the territory and still contains a famous library.

The vast stone structure is built around a large rectangular courtyard in which some remaining columns testify to the presence of an earlier surrounding cloister. It also contains a staircase leading to an underground corridor, referred to variously as a prison or as a cistern, if the latter then this may well have been either the tank or underground reservoir associated with an original temple. The exterior walls of the building are lime-washed, but the interior of the courtyard is painted pink, against which the touches of white stand out dramatically.

One side of the courtyard is occupied by the great, recently restored church which has a single nave and a wooden ceiling similar to that of the Church of Bom Jesus in Old Goa but without the supporting brackets. The walls are plain white with the exception of a richly carved pulpit which juts out from the southern wall. A large barrel-vaulted apse contains the High altar and is profusely decorated and gilded, the great altar-piece itself containing a series of niches with statues of the saints, while the side walls have a number of cartouches containing paintings of episodes from the lives of the saints. Each of these cartouches is framed by angels within a luxuriantly foliate border, the same treatment being given to the spandrels fronting the apse vault.

Other parts of this immense building have decorative touches, but generally it has a more functional feeling. It is still in use as a Seminary, and the central courtyard was marked out with lines for some form of recreation for the students.

Both Pilar and Rachol are great ecclesiastical institutions but, particularly in the Old Conquests, churches are everywhere, and it becomes almost invidious to select specific examples. The late seventeenth century Church of St Anna at Tallauli (see cover illustration), with its sublime vault resting on a series of entablatures and capitals designed to give the illusion of rising curves, is perhaps the quintessential example of Indian Baroque, whilst the great Church of the Holy Spirit at Margao (pl. 25), with its classical Goan facade, is one of the most majestic. Originally built in 1564 it was completely rebuilt in 1675 and is now a particularly grand example of Goa's white-painted churches. It dominates a large square around which are a series of fine town houses while in the centre is a magnificent example of the monumental crosses (col. pl. 24; see also pl. 26 for the cross at Chandor) which are such a feature of the Goan landscape, in this case standing alongside a superb mango tree.

The church of Loutulim (pl. 27) with its single tower, or the beautiful church at Calangute with the artificial grotto facing it, all of these and many others, some of which simply line the road in delightful anonymity, constantly delight the eye at every turn (see, for example, pls. 28–29). The Church of the Rosary at Saligao (col. pl. 25) deserves particular mention as being the only Gothic church in the territory, and also the Church at Teracol because it is set in the middle of a fortress, and thus leads on to the next architectural theme.

Throughout their sea-borne empire the Portuguese needed to build a series of forts to defend their coastal territories. The first of these was built in West Africa on the Gold Coast in 1480 at a site which the Portuguese christened Mina, the Mine, because the whole area appeared to be rich in gold. Fort St George 'da Mina' thus became the model for all the major Portuguese forts and eventually, for the Dutch and British as well, although considerable advances were made in fortress construction during the late sixteenth century which were also incorporated.

25 The Church of the Holy Spirit in Margao with a monumental cross in the square

26 Monumental cross at Chandor

27 The Parish Church of Loutulim

28 Church near Loutulim with the signs of the sun and moon on the facade

Giovanni Battista Cairati, an Italian from Milan, known in Portuguese as João Baptista Cairato, was a leading military architect and, after the union of the Portuguese and Spanish empires in 1580, he was sent to the east by Philip II to redesign many of the fortresses. His principal achievements were at Daman and Bassein, although he also worked at Manar in Ceylon, Malacca, Muscat, and Hormuz, and in 1593 he designed Fort Jesus in Mombassa shortly before his death in Goa in 1596. Although he was not officially associated with the construction of any of the forts in Goa itself, undoubtedly many of his ideas would have been incorporated into any subsequent rebuilding.

In India a chain of forts linked the various Portuguese territories, and where, as in Goa and the Province of the North, the territory was reasonably deep, there were forts at significant sites around the boundaries and for defence inside major towns. During the Maratha wars it was the inspired but desperate defence of the forts in the Province of the North which earned the epithet 'Warriors like the Portuguese' from the awe-struck enemy, and when the enemy attacked Goa itself it was only the existence of the forts on the north shore of the Mandovi which kept the harbour open and enabled the territory to survive. As the territory was extended at the end of the eighteenth century more coastal forts were established, but very few further inland, only at very strategic river crossings and such places, while the jungle to the east along the foothills of the Western Ghats was left comparatively undefended.

29 Village church in Salcete

A number of these forts still remain and constitute an interesting addition to the history of Portuguese India. Teracol fort (*col. pl. 26*, plan 1) is the most northerly and actually occupies a small enclave on the northern side of the Teracol river which forms the state boundary. Like all the forts it is situated on a piece of high ground, in this case a headland commanding a fine view of the ocean and at the same time enabling the fort to guard the entrance to the estuary and the harbour. It is not a large fort and was primarily designed to control the sea and the estuary, and not against a land-based attack, although the walls are strong and rise sheer from an excavated dry moat, with a series of decorative turrets at each corner to command either field of fire.

The chapel (*col. pls. 28–29*) within the fort is comparatively large and probably catered for the needs of any nearby community. It has a classical late Goan facade with the central pediment rising higher than the two towers, the roof of the single nave being concealed behind it. At present the fort is used as a Tourist Hostel and provides a romantic base from which to survey the northern section of the territory, or simply to enjoy the quiet beach and the fishing.

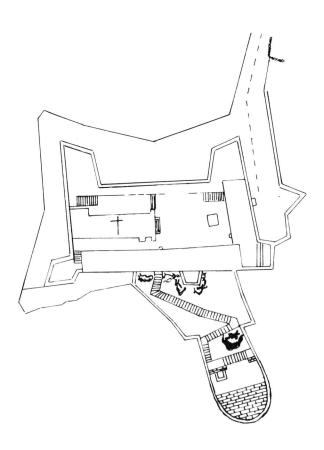

Plan 1 Teracol fort

30 Chapora fort on its headland which overlooks Vagator beach

The next southerly estuary is that of the river Chapora, and the ruins of Chapora fort (pl. 30) rise high above the river on the southern headland. Initially this fort was known as Shapur, when it was built by the 'Adil Shah, and was subsequently the headquarters of Akbar, son of Aurangzeb the last great Mughal emperor. At the foot of the fortress is a natural mineral spring which was originally outside the walls, but it was later incorporated within the defences and linked by a tunnel to the main fortress.

The fort dominates Vagator beach which, along with the nearby Anjuna beach have long been names to conjure with in the annals of the more relaxed and possibly, although not necessarily more impecunious travellers, who have been aware of the beauties and advantages of Goa for many years. Recently with the opening of a new beach resort at Vagator, the needs of some of the other travellers have also been catered for, while the fort looms benignly over all.

Perhaps the greatest transformation has taken place in the largest of all the coastal forts, Fort Aguada (col. pl. 30, plan 2), which now plays host to one of the best hotels in the territory on the leeward side, while the main fortress buildings on the estuary house the Central Jail. On one side of the headland the Nerul River flows into the Mandovi estuary, and a moat was dug to link the coastal bastion to the river making the entire headland into an island (see pl. 31). Because of a large sweet

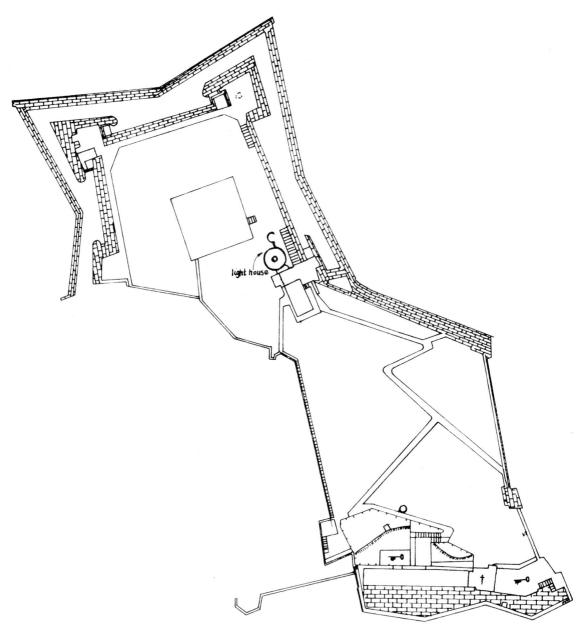

Plan 2 Aguada fort

water well, now within the courtyard of the jail, the island was totally self-sufficient, in fact ships would dock there to obtain a supply of freshwater both leaving and entering Goa harbour.

With its series of bastions and heavily defended walls (*col. pl. 31*, pl. 32) the fort was the strongest in Goa. The main fortifications are still intact and in use, but the majority of the outer bastions have crumbled with the exception of one of the great

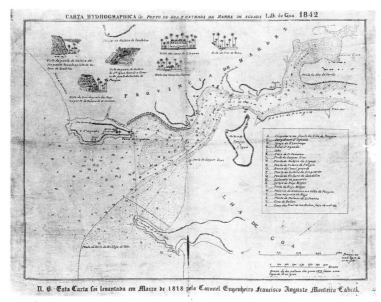

31 An 1818 map of the entrance to the Mandovi showing the position of Fort Aguada, Reis Magos, the Fort of Cabo and Panjim itself, connected to Raibandar by the multiple-arched bridge-causeway (courtesy Directorate of Historical Archives)

bastions on the northern side of the headland facing the Arabian Sea, which stretches out into the sea and provides a sheltered harbour. This has now been restored which helps to visualize how the fort must have looked when only Fort Aguada and Reis Magos, the other fort on the Mandovi to the east, remained of the northern territory when it was being attacked by the allies of the Marathas.

Built in 1612, the fort contained 79 guns which were so sited as to cover all possible approaches. The central area of the fort rises to 80 metres, upon which eminence the church of St Lawrence was built in 1630 by the then Viceroy the Count of Linhares. Nearby a beautiful 13 metre high lighthouse (pl. 33) was added in 1864 which still dominates the fortress area although a modern lighthouse now does the work. One of the first lighthouses to be built in Asia, its rotating lantern was visible for 26 miles.

Immediately opposite Fort Aguada on the headland to the south of the Mandovi was the fortress of Cabo which was begun as early as 1540 to guard the entrance to the river. This site has had a chequered history, a Franciscan monastery being built alongside the fort in 1594, and when the British troops entered Goa during the Napoleonic wars they garrisoned the Cabo fort and built themselves barracks which were subsequently demolished by the Portuguese. The monastery was later given to the archbishop of Goa as a residence but was soon taken over as a country seat by the governor-general, and has now become the official residence of the lieutenant-governor. The elegant verandahs of Raj Niwas still command a panoramic view of the entrance to the Mandovi, although no longer with the same intent, while the lawns slope down to the ruins of the fortress walls. Inside this elegant mansion still contains and uses the fine crockery and porcelain adorned with the Portuguese coat of arms. Legend has it that this is because the last governor was too much of a gentleman to give the order to destroy things so that the present occupants are able to enjoy the specially designed eighteenth and nineteenth century Chinese export ware belonging to the previous incumbents.

32 Fort Aguada; one of the remaining bastions overlooking the sea

33 Fort Aguada; the elegant nineteenth century lighthouse within the fortress area

All that remains of the fortress of Gaspar Dias, built a mile and a half along the bank to the east and destroyed during the mutiny of 1835, is the great cannon which looked across to the fort of Reis Magos and would have provided a most effective cross-fire to the guns of the fort. Gaspar Dias and Reis Magos were thus the second line of defence for the capital should an enemy manage to sail past Aguada and Cabo, and the walls of Reis Magos (pl. 34, plan 3) still dominate the inner harbour. A strangely X-shaped fortress with two inner courtyards, it was begun in 1551 on the site of a Hindu temple. Its turreted walls are still in perfect condition and, like Fort Aguada, it also serves as a prison. Alongside its walls is a delightful church, also dedicated to the Reis Magos, which was one of the first churches to be constructed north of the Mandovi as early as 1555. The coast rises swiftly at this point so that the church, like the fort, is on high ground and approached by a flight of very steep steps, while behind it nestles the walled parish graveyard on a still higher level.

Apart from the massive series of curtain walls and fortified gateways, a major feature of these fortifications was a series of cylindrical turrets which still adorn most of the exterior angles. In addition to their pleasing aesthetic aspect they also enabled the sentries to dominate the surrounding countryside, and provided a position from which they were able to sweep any approaching enemy with a murderous cross-fire, particularly useful when warding off the attacks of the Marathas.

Almost nothing remains of the other most important fort of the territory, that of Marmagao which was situated on the southern headland of the Zuari river, and to which the Viceroy moved the non-combatants from Old Goa when the city itself was menaced in 1683. Aguada and Marmagao between them thus controlled the great double estuary and were consequently of vital importance. As the Conde de Sandomil expressed it while he was Viceroy, they 'form the throat through which these islands and provinces breathe. They are therefore to be preserved even if the said provinces are lost, in the interests of the security of the capital . . .' At one stage a disastrous attempt was made to move the capital to Marmagao from Old Goa which only served to precipitate the destruction of the old capital, but today any remains are covered by the developments around the town of Vasco da Gama.

The southernmost fort is that of Cabo de Rama, so called because Rama, the eponymous hero of the Hindu epic the *Ramayana*, is said to have lived in the area with his wife Sita during their period of exile. The cape on which it is situated is naturally defensible and needed little fortification except on the landward side. Here an impressive wall still divides the area of the fort from the neighbouring village, the gatehouse still rearing up in the centre (pl. 35), but little remains inside the large enclosed area except a church and a few ruined walls. Like a number of other forts, it had its origins in pre-Portuguese times and was only acquired in 1763 and, also like some of the others, it ended its days as a prison. Nowadays it has little to interest any visitor who is willing to brave the two-hour walk from the nearest road and is best seen by boat where distance lends enchantment to its straggling ruins.

Of the inland forts that of St Estevam is possibly one of the most interesting if only for its historical connections. This was the fort which was captured by the Marathas in 1683 and which nearly led to the death of the Viceroy in an attempt to

34 The fortress of Reis Magos overlooking the estuary of the Mandovi

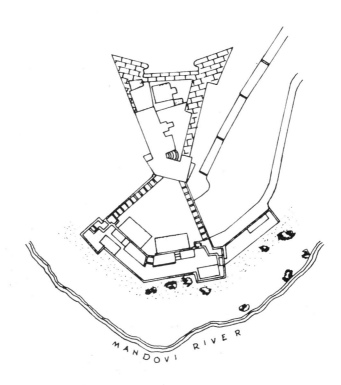

Plan 3 Reis Magos fort

recapture it, shortly before he resigned the direction of the state into the hands of St Francis Xavier. The fort is on Santo Estevam island and looks north across a branch of the Mandovi towards Bicholim. It follows the contours of the hill on which it sits, and is consequently roughly triangular in shape. Much of the outer walls are still standing and also the main gate, which was approached up a ramp carved out of the rock and across an excavated dry moat, presumably by some form of drawbridge. It suffers from no particular architectural pretensions, but gives the impression that it could have held out for longer had any of the guards been awake.

As with most of the other forts St Estevao emerges from the rock itself, that is to say that part of the defences are excavated and it is the excavated stone which was used to construct the walls of the fort. At the time possibly large sections would have been lime-plastered as a protection against the climate, certainly the inner sections and the church if any, as can be seen in Teracol. It is less certain that the outer walls were so treated, but certainly the fort at Elmina in West Africa, which gave the model to so many others, is lime-plastered, so that it is very probable. The present denuded state of the ruins gives them a much more organic feel, and they almost seem a natural phenomenon as the same coloured walls rise out of the rock, only the chiselled architectural details revealing the hand of man.

Not so with the other great Portuguese architectural legacy, the palatial houses and mansions which are to be found all over the territory, an elegant witness to the luxurious standards which prevailed during the times of splendour. Most of these old manors were built in the early eighteenth century at a time when Portugal attained a degree of prosperity unknown since the restoration of 1640. This was due to the wealth which poured in from the gold and precious stones of Brazil, and the Royal fifth levied on this gave the monarchy an independent source of income. Goa also undoubtedly benefited from this New World wealth, and the lavish profusion of the Royal Court was amply reflected in the Viceregal.

35 The ruined gatehouse of the most southerly fortress on Cabo de Rama

At the same time a number of Goans were also themselves accumulating large fortunes abroad, mainly in the Portuguese provinces in Africa, a trend which still continues in the present day, and this wealth was used to build the great mansions at home. Other Goans held high positions under the Portuguese and were rewarded with large grants of land as well as earning a reasonable official stipend. Estates thus grew and were nurtured within a comparatively small group of families, most of whom inter-married at one stage or other, so that the majority of the old families are related to each other. Large families were also usual with outbuildings and dependencies necessary to house the regiment of people required to maintain the estate, hence the scale on which so many of these mansions were built.

Grandeur was not however limited to the size of the establishment but was an integral part of the furnishings. Mirrors and chandeliers were brought from Venice and Bohemia, tapestries were imported from Spain and Portugal, porcelain was brought from China in huge quantities, and silks and brocades came from neighbouring Indian centres. Most of the actual furniture was made locally, but was superbly carved out of rare woods expressly imported for the purpose. Here the native Indian taste expressed itself and one sees great sets of chairs and tables covered with a rich profusion of carving that leaves no space undecorated.

Fundamentally these houses maintain a European sense of space and form, although, like the church architecture, within a Goan tradition. The main rooms are all on the first floor, the 'piano nobile' syndrome, with all the service rooms on the ground floor. Houses however almost never went above two storeys, and the general appearance is one of sprawling width, and a feeling that the house could go on growing indefinitely in any direction. Some of course have facades of almost classical simplicity, but then the feeling is one of depth, of the house meandering ever deeper into the estate.

The materials used and the techniques employed in the Goan vernacular architecture are not fundamentally different from others in the general Konkan region in that all use laterite blocks for walls and verandah pillars with wooden beam roofs and Mangalore tiles. Goan architecture however adds several distinctive touches which distinguish it from all neighbouring constructions. The most obvious of these is the balcão, the columned porch, usually with a pyramidal roof, which juts out from the house front and with its stalled sides and seats provides a meeting place and observation point. Many of the great family mansions lack this adjunct or replace it with a broad verandah along the entire front of the house, but in all other houses it is one of the most easily distinguishable features.

The typical Goan house could in fact be described as having a central rectangular core with a high-pitched Mangalore tiled roof. Around this central core is a verandah which either completely encircles it or lies along the front only, and can be either open or walled, thus creating a further series of rooms around the central ones. The tiled roof of this extension is pitched against the wall of the central core slightly below the main roof which projects over the lower, giving an elegant two-tiered effect and enabling the architect to draw attention to the decorative cornice.

These projecting roofs of Goan buildings are generally supported by a cornice formed of rows of cantilevered Mangalore tiles. These curved tiles which are such a feature of all the roofs in western India have here been used to create an extra art form which gives the roofs an aesthetic finish and a rounded solid appearance quite distinct from the more usual simple roof projection. This two-tiered effect with a further projecting porch or balcão, would have been the form originally taken by the Safa Mosque before its partial destruction as is evidenced by the columns which surround it.

Window designs tend to follow the Baroque, with elegant curves which are often accentuated by the use of coloured washes and are reflected in the wrought iron balconies and verandahs which form an integral part of the facades. This love of curves is also manifested in the relief plaster mouldings which surmount most doors and windows and lend an exuberant Rococo touch to otherwise restrained classical facades.

Another peculiarly Goan institution is the substitution of translucent oyster shells for glass panes in the windows. The outer shell is removed so that the nacre is left and squares of this are fitted into wooden frames, still remaining in many of the older houses. Unfortunately this is now a dying art and replacements are therefore almost impossible, but the ones which survive give a warm, filtered light to rooms which would otherwise be washed by the full glare of the sun. This is a very old tradition in Goa, being noted by the Frenchman François Pyrard at the beginning of the seventeenth century. He said that such windows gave as much light as paper windows or horn lanterns, but were not so transparent as glass.

In all the Christian homes of Goa the main reception rooms were the recipients of the greatest love and care. Wealth and attention were lavished on them so that they could be the fitting background for the formal entertaining which was such an integral part of the stately colonial life-style.

The other great common factor in Goan houses was the incorporation of a family shrine or chapel. Many of these were worthy of the splendour of the houses they graced, complete with richly carved altars housing beautifully painted ivory statues, others were of more modest proportions, but all houses contained some form of oratory which was the actual heart of the family. This concept of a private family shrine manifestly derives from the mainstream of Hindu Indian tradition, and indeed the same craftsmen would have been called in to decorate both the Hindu and Christian religious buildings, both private and public, and ultimately all drew on the same artistic sources. Some of the attendant figures became angels and cherubs in their Christian manifestations, but the same rich Indian aesthetic pervades both.

All of these traditions came together in some of the great houses which still remain to astonish the modern traveller with the varied richness of Goan life. A grand Portuguese style imported from the splendours of eighteenth century Lisbon was achieved with distinctive Goan workmanship which integrated a lively Indian feeling into the whole and bound it to the land. This harmonious symbiosis between East and West is essentially and most successfully found in Goan homes which are the most accurate reflectors of this life style.

One such is the beautiful Miranda house at Loutulim which is also one of the oldest having been first built around 1700. The facade (pls. 36–37), with its regular series of rectangular windows is almost severe in its classicism, relieved only by the first floor balconies and the balustraded stone terrace. The interior belies this somewhat austere impression and revolves about the inner courtyard garden which

36 The main facade of the Miranda house
in Loutulim

37 A detail of the facade of the Miranda house in Loutulim

has deep verandahs (pl. 38) on two sides where most of the living is led. This is a characteristic of almost all the houses and reflects the Indian tradition, to group the house around a central courtyard, with shady verandahs forming a vital part of the house structure. The food preparation and dining rooms also tend to lie at the back of the house, possibly following another Indian tendency which is that the meal forms the final part of an evening. Entertaining leads up to the meal which is the culmination, unlike the usual Western concept of the meal being the prelude to an evening's conversation. The final move back into the dining area would thus also signal the final stage of an evening's entertainment, all of which had been designed to take place in the front reception part of the house.

The Miranda house is somewhat unusual in that the principal entertaining rooms are all on the ground floor, the drawing room being in the front and leading directly on to the balustraded terrace. The majority of the bedrooms are also on the ground floor, as is the spacious private chapel. A staircase leads directly from the front hall to the first floor and the great banqueting hall which occupies almost the entire upper floor overlooking the front garden. The library opens off this and fills the west end of the floor, while beyond a moveable partition at the other end of the hall access can be gained to the principal bedroom suite.

The present owners have added a great many new decorative touches to the house, using colour in an excitingly bold way, and mixing richly printed Indian fabrics with the more austere lines of the old furniture in very successful combinations. The chapel (*col. pl. 32*) has been given brilliant pillar box red doors and ceiling which creates a warm reflected glow in this airy room, while another room has been turned into a snug hideout with deeply cushioned chairs and banquettes bright with Indian prints. Elsewhere in the house the cherished antiques are reflected on the polished tiled floors, and the old machila, an original Goan wooden palanquin or carrying chair, still sits in its own special niche under the main staircase.

Loutulim is a very old village, and the area around it has a number of fine old mansions, many of which are beautifully maintained in a traditional manner. One such is the Salvador Costa house which has now been divided in two sections because of the number of heirs to the property. One part of the house contains a wealth of fine furniture which, along with a number of family paintings and antique mirrors on the walls, and exquisite Bohemian glass chandeliers, create a perfect traditional setting against the pale blue walls (see pls. 39–40). A spacious verandah (pl. 41) runs along the front of the house providing an area for relaxation and conversation, two favourite Goan pastimes, and the back looks onto a central courtyard garden.

38 The verandah at the heart of the Miranda house

39 The salon of the Salvador Costa house

40 A magnificent carved wardrobe in the Salvador Costa house

Both the Miranda and de Costa houses are outside the village and set in their own grounds, but similar houses are to be found in the centres of towns and villages as well. In the middle of Loutulim village the Roque Caetan Miranda house has adapted the expansive Goan traditional forms to the confines of a more urban setting. The approach to the house leads down from the mainstreet through shady trees which help keep the house deliciously cool. The chapel is a large room off the entrance hall on the ground floor, but the main living rooms are on the first floor. The salon which occupies the front of the house, with finely fretted french windows leading onto a series of balconies, is another large room with furnishings which date back to the foundation of the house in 1815. The carved wooden chairs all have the initials RCM as the centrepiece of the design on their backs like some heraldic device, their elegant black forms making patterns against the white walls, like the wrought-iron balustrades against the sunlight. All of this, including the gleam from the two Bohemian glass chandeliers, is reflected in the highly polished wooden floor, which again seems to be a feature in these stately homes.

27 *Panjim*

29 Teracol cross

31 Looking across one of the remaining bastions of Fort Aguada to Calangute beach from the Fort Aguada hotel

32 The chapel of the Miranda house at Loutulim

34 The temple of Shri Saptakoteshwara at Narve in Bicholim

36 *Dawn on Calangute beach*

40 *The tank at the temple of Shri Manguesh*

42 *Panjim waterfront*

44 Colva houses

45 Fort Aguada from across Calangute beach

46 *Fort Aguada hotel*

48 Mayem Lake

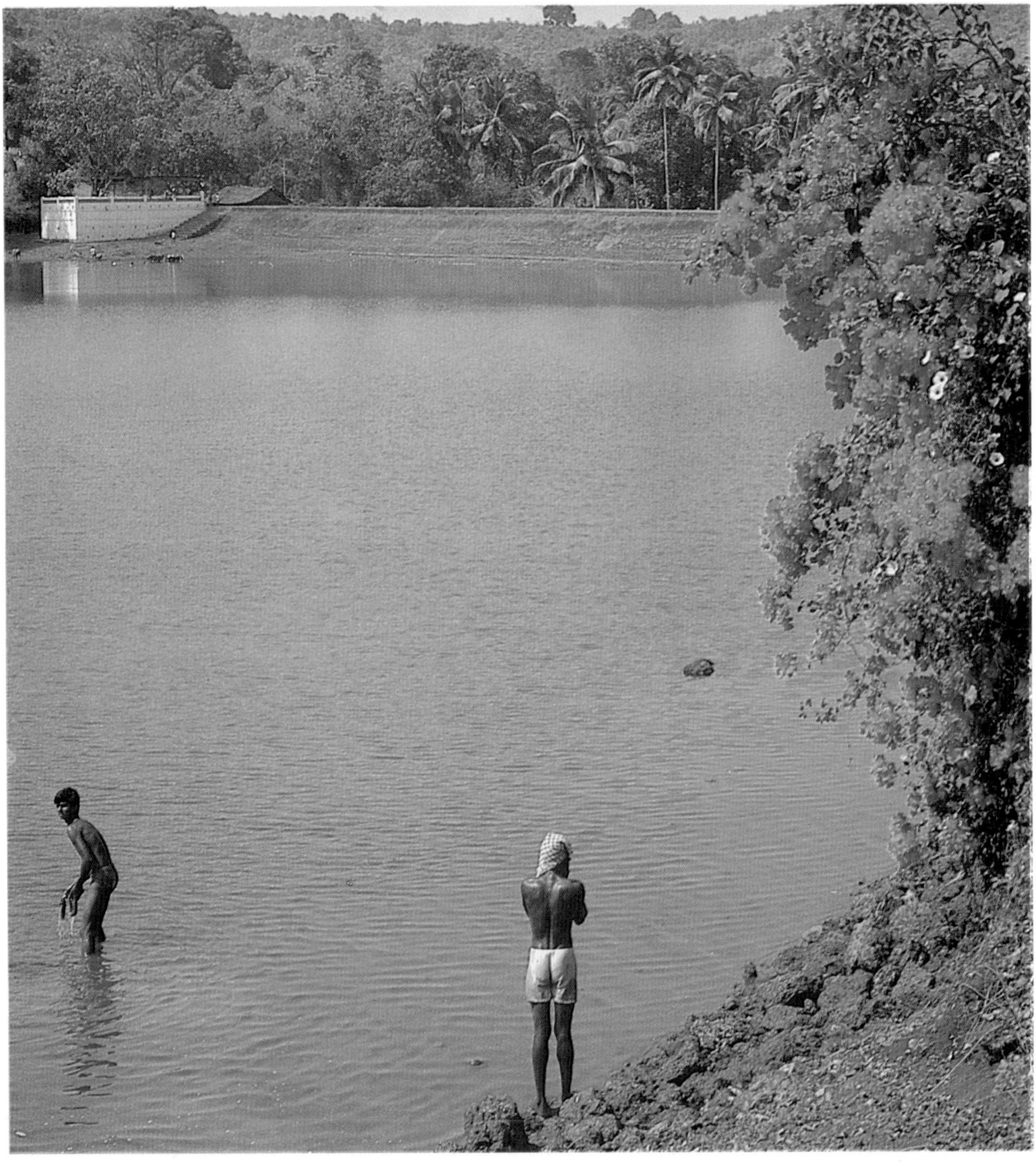

One of the grandest urban houses is the stately da Silva house (plan 4) in Margao known as Seven Shoulders. This name refers to the seven gables which used to adorn the three hundred year old house of which only three still remain. Now only a third of its former size the house is still capacious, and has managed to retain the major reception rooms, although the enormous old salon which was capable of holding 200 people has been divided. The two-storeyed facade is approached up two flights of steps (pl. 42) which neatly divide the front terrace, and is painted pink with the architectural details picked out in white. The effect is very elegant, with the wrought-iron balconies on the first floor, and the whole crowned by the remaining three high-pitched gabled roofs.

A magnificent staircase leads up to the first floor and at the half-way stage facing the entrance is the beautiful chapel behind wrought-iron doors. This little chapel is more in the nature of an oratory and contains some very fine wood carving set off against the pale blue and gold altar-piece through which the light streams from the window behind, outlining the delicate tracery around the statue of St Anna. This was one of the first families in Goa to obtain the privilege of having mass celebrated in their private chapel, so that the chapel is also an historical monument.

The reception rooms on the first floor house a very fine collection of carved rosewood furniture, family portraits and paintings, as well as the outsize mirrors which were often imported at enormous cost from Europe along with the glass chandeliers. Cabinets also contain some of the family's collection of glass and porcelain, a collection which is maintained by the present owner, the ninth generation of the family to live in the house. The little courtyard at the rear, around which the rest of the house is grouped, is almost bisected by the chapel which protrudes into it, but is full of flowers, and forms a tranquil garden centre for this town house fronting, as it does, onto a main road.

One of the largest and finest collections of old Goan furniture is in the Vicente João de Figueiredo house, the great sprawling front of which was added 150 years ago to this three hundred year old country mansion. Three enormous salons encircle the inevitable courtyard garden, the fourth side having a more family-sized and relaxed reception room, although even this contains fine furniture. The salons however have some of the finest Goan carved furniture in existence, each piece lovingly polished and cared for by the present owner who is a most charming hostess but understandably worried about maintaining such a superb collection in its entirety.

Elaborately carved rosewood furniture was a great feature of Goan houses, and some of the designs reached unimaginable degrees of complication. This, combined with an Indian 'Horror vacui', produced some amazing pieces of furniture, chairs, tables, consoles, cupboards, which were in themselves works of art. Many of these were also upholstered with the finest European silks and brocades, as well as exquisite examples of Indian silks, and are in consequence, not merely museum pieces as works of art, but of vital historical importance for the history of fabrics as well as the history of furniture.

The collection in the Figueiredo house covers the three hundred year period of the house's history and contains outstanding examples of each style. These are all arranged within the rooms as they would have been in more spacious times, and there is no sense of anything approaching a museum. The rooms are used and lived

41 The facade of the Salvador Costa house in Loutulim

42 The facade of the stately da Silva house in Margao with its three gables

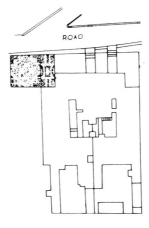

Plan 4 da Silva house

in, and the care with which the furniture is treated is a reflection of the good taste with which the house is maintained.

The delicacy of the carving on the furniture is also continued on the woodwork details of the house itself (pl. 43), and as with so many of the these buildings, the windows are lovingly set in intricate patterns, and the carved wooden balustrade around the interior courtyard has an inter-laced design with a centre of open painted flowers. Set against the rich green plants of the lower-sited garden, or seen through the luxuriant bougainvillea which fills the terrace in front of the house, these details add a dimension of quality to all these houses which is so rarely to be found nowadays when time and speed are of the essence.

The enormous Menezes Braganza house in Chandor has parts dating back to the sixteenth century when the family was still Hindu, although the greater part of this small palace was built in the late eighteenth century with a further addition in the nineteenth. The front of the house (pl. 44) is very long, and its two-storeys conceal two courtyard gardens divided by the main staircase which rises rather grandly from the centre front hall. All of the reception halls are on the first floor as usual, and form a range of rooms whose magnificence would be envied in many of Europe's great houses.

The great salon (*col. pl. 33*) is especially fine, and has a number of chandeliers above a polished tile floor on which stand pale-blue upholstered eighteenth century French-style chairs. At the far end of this salon is an exquisite little withdrawing room containing some of the family's collection of porcelain and fine furniture. A central sitting room leads to the library. This is the largest and finest private collection in Goa and contains over 5,000 volumes in various languages. It belonged to Luis de Menezes Braganza the great journalist and nationalist, and it is still maintained as it was when he was using it. The library opens on to another long drawing room which leads to the beautiful dining room. This again is a huge room, almost as large as the great salon, with a series of latticed french doors leading to a covered verandah which runs along the front of the house. The small private chapel is centrally situated within the house and has a Baroque gilded altar-piece and a fine series of silver candlesticks on the altar itself.

43 The courtyard of the Figueiredo house showing the fretted woodwork in the windows

44 The enormous front of the Menezes Braganza house in Chandor

45 An elegantly furnished hallway in the Menezes Braganza house

The whole house has been conceived on the grand scale, with rooms and corridors (pl. 45) opening out of each other in a way which would have been perfectly understood in the Europe of that time. The bedrooms and other private rooms were all to the back around the courtyards, while all the servants and domestic quarters were on the ground floor leaving this stunning series of rooms undisturbed by any domestic problems. The more relaxed Indian attitudes allowed an easier and more comfortable existence than was possible in parts of Europe, certainly in the etiquette-ridden courts of Spain, but life was certainly very expansive and a princely hospitality was customary and is still an integral part of the Goan character.

All of these houses are in the southern province of Salcete with Margao as its capital where landowners still have vast estates of paddy fields and coconut groves and where the great house is a natural centre, but there are also major estates in the other provinces. The Souza Gonçalves house in Guirim has already been mentioned as the headquarters for the Infante Don Afonso in the late nineteenth century. This white-painted house was built two hundred years ago by Pedro Inacio de Souza, a government official, whose only daughter married a Gonçalves, and the subsequent descendants retained both names.

Both the dining room and the chapel are on the ground floor of this house, the chapel having one of the few Gothic style altar-pieces to be found in Goa and where recently permission has been given to have mass celebrated. An unusual staircase leads to the upper floor with each step hewn out of a single piece of granite. The salon is also unusual in that not only is the white painted ceiling made from teak wood, but also the furniture. This is different from the more traditional rosewood furniture and is designed along lighter, more simple lines, having more than a touch of Sheraton, particularly about the chairs.

The ground floor also houses the original kitchens, with space for vast fires which are still occasionally used. A more modern kitchen provides for the general needs of the family, but the deep fires in a splendidly smoke-blackened room, the light gleaming from copper cauldrons, gives a marvellous impression of life below stairs. This area opens onto the central courtyard which is functional rather than aesthetic, and leads one back to the entrance hall.

This tradition of building magnificent houses, often with money originally made outside Goa, did not cease with the nineteenth century as can be seen in the beautiful Albuquerque mansion at Anjuna. This house was built in the 1920s by a Goan who had practised as a doctor in Zanzibar, but who, like almost all Goans, wanted to retire to his homeland. The house is large and imposing with the usual two storeys, the facade being flanked by octagonal towers with tiled roofs, but the side having an arched verandah with a similar arched terrace above, the double arching effect more reminiscent of East Africa than Goa. The house is painted bright yellow with white woodwork and balustrading, a combination found in a number of Goan houses which looks very attractive with the Mangalore tile roofs and is still used today.

THE HINDU CONTRIBUTION TO GOAN ARCHITECTURE

With the exception of the beautifully carved stone Kadamba temple at Tambdi Surla, which has already been described, there are almost no old Hindu temples left in Goa of the hundreds which once existed there. Most of these would have been wooden or mud-brick structures designed as a home for a cult statue and would have been destroyed easily, but the all too rare fragments of carved stone which are found occasionally indicate that there must have been a number of other fine temples. Unfortunately the area of the Old Conquests was always the richest and most powerful, and most of the finest temples would have been grouped in this region, and it was here that the wrath of the Church and the Inquisition were felt most strongly so that none survived.

What has survived are a number of the most important cult statues which were saved by their devoted followers and taken out of the reach of the Inquisition, eventually to be returned when the religious persecution was ended. Thus although the temple housing the statue may be of comparatively recent construction the statue in worship may well be one that escaped the conflagration and has been in worship for many centuries indeed.

Most of the major Hindu deities are represented in Goa although sometimes the names by which they are known are not those commonly given them in the West. In many instances these represent particular attributes or aspects of the deity which are those which the worshippers particularly desire to appease or propitiate, or other aspects which they feel should be encouraged. Thus Shiva is worshipped in a great many places and the lingam, the image by which he is mainly represented, is to be found throughout the territory, but he is invoked under many names such as Saptakoteshwara, Manguesh, Naguesh, as well as under his more terrible form in the name of Bhairava or a Betal. His consort, the goddess Parvati, is also known as Shantadurga, and as such is the Great Mother or the Goddess of Peace, while under her terrible form she is known as Kali, although there are not many temples in Goa under this guise. Vishnu also occurs as Narayan or Vitthala, but can also be depicted in the form of any of his nine 'avatars' or incarnations. His consort, the Goddess Lakshmi, goddess of wealth and prosperity, is however venerated throughout the territory by everyone as Mahalakshmi, Mahalsa, or Gajalakshmi. In addition to these deities all of the other principal ones are to be found either with their own temples or having shrines in association with other temples.

Each of these deities and the many and various forms under which the main gods appear, all have their own iconography and are physically represented in a very precise manner. Despite the Muslim and Christian periods of destruction Goa is rich in such representations, and although a number of them have been gathered together in the Archaeological Museum in Old Goa, the majority are still in worship and constitute a strong continuous tradition, going back in a number of instances to the sixth and seventh centuries of this era.

Each town or village had its main deity but to these would be added a number of other affiliated deities who would have been especially venerated in that area. Thus Ganesh, or as he is more widely known in South India, Ganapathi, was the principal deity of Ela before it became the city of Goa, but in addition the goddess Saraswati, the goddess of learning, also had a shrine there. One of the very rare images of this goddess which dates from the mediaeval period, has also been found near a Shiva temple in the north of the territory near Pernem, and since temples of this goddess are very rare, the existence of possibly two sites in Goa during the mediaeval period would imply a great devotion to learning on the part of the Kadambas.

Temples of Saraswati's consort Brahma are even more rare, he is usually worshipped in association with either Shiva or Vishnu, the three together forming the main Hindu triad. Apparently there was a temple to this god at Carambolim which was destroyed at the time of the conquest, but the very fine image was saved and was transferred in 1541 to a village in the northwest of the present Goan territory called Cormoli, where it was re-erected in a small temple and is still in worship. Another image of this god dating from the seventh century was found abandoned near a small village in Pernem district.

An image of Surya, the sun god, was found in a village called Cudnem in Bicholim district, which apparently dates back to the seventh or eighth century. The image does not stand in a chariot as is usual, but is flanked by two attendant figures of almost equal height, the whole concept indicating a close relationship with early Kushan figures of the sun god. The existence of this figure indicated that the sun god was worshipped in Goa in early times, but there is currently no temple to him in the territory.

When the depredations of the Inquisition forced many of the devotees to remove the images from Goan territory for safety, a number of the most important were only taken as far as Ponda just over the border, presumably so that their adherents could still visit their shrines, and the beneficent influence of the cult statues would still be felt. As a result some of the most important temples in Goa are now to be found near Ponda, and date their foundation back to the sixteenth century, the shrine of Shri Shantadurga at Kavalem having recently enjoyed its fourth centenary amid great celebrations.

Although many of these temples date their foundations to the sixteenth century, the buildings as they are at present are the result of a number of rebuildings, some in the late seventeenth and eighteenth centuries while the areas were still under the control of the Maratha rulers, the others after they had become part of the Portuguese territory at the end of the eighteenth century. At that time the authority of the Inquisition was at an end and the rich Hindu merchants of Goa were able once again to build temples more appropriate to the wealth and standing of their community.

Saptakoteshwara is a particular aspect of the god Shiva, and is worshipped either in the form of a linga or in human form as Bhairava. He acquired this name from having defeated two demons leading an army of seven times ten million, or seven crores, and so is Lord of seven crores, Saptakoteshwara in Sanskrit. This deity was particularly patronised by the Kadamba rulers, and the main temple was at Narve on Diwadi island. After the destruction of this temple the linga was hidden and eventually smuggled across to Bicholim district to its present site, which was renamed Narve out of respect.

It was a particularly holy image and the Portuguese were forced to pass a number of laws at the behest of the Inquisition forbidding people taking part in its festivals. In 1668, when this whole area was under the rule of the Marathas, Sivaji built a new and much enlarged temple (*col. pl. 34*) for the god, which is basically that now in existence. The style is distinctly Goan and patently owes a great deal to European architectural influence. The shallow dome of the sanctuary rests on an octagonal drum which rises out of a sloping tiled roof, in front of which the main temple resembles a nave with two lower side aisles. The arcaded front hall is attached to the temple like a large portico, and in front of the temple the stambha pillar is mounted on a stepped dais. With the water tank in front of it, this particular form of temple, allowing for minor alterations, is the standard Goan temple, and has multiplied considerably, especially in the area of the New Conquests.

In 1738 the Marathas were again attacking Goa, so successfully that they almost took it over completely, and in that year the Maratha ruler Shahu, grandson of Sivaji, was persuaded by one of his ministers to rebuild the temple of Shantadurga at Kavale (*col. pl. 35*), and this is now the main shrine of the deity in Goa. The image was originally brought from Kavlesi in southern Salcete district in the sixteenth century, and presumably some shelter was erected for it at that time, but the major construction cannot be earlier than Shahu's building.

The drum of the sanctuary dome is higher than that of Saptakoteshwara, having three stages, two of which contain windows. There are also a number of transepts and side chapels which may well be accretions over the centuries. As one of the most important temples it has naturally attracted considerable donations, and many of these undoubtedly took the form of building additions. After the accession of Ponda to Goa in the late eighteenth century this building activity must have heightened, and a great deal of what exists at the present day is the result of nineteenth century construction which was strongly influenced by current European taste. This does not however detract from the beauty of the temple complex, and it is very probable that the major part of the main temple dates from the Shahu period.

The architectural style of these temples is almost totally European and owes very little apart from the plan to Indian influence. The dome above the sanctuary set on an octagonal tower ornamented with pilasters and balustrades, is purely Baroque in inspiration. A certain Indian opulence has been achieved in some instances by the addition of bright colours and kneeling elephants as in the Shri Kamaxi temple at Shiroda (pl. 46), but the brilliant white in which the majority are painted makes the European origin even more strongly accentuated.

If the temple dome has a European Baroque inspiration the same can be said of the other major feature which is peculiar to Goan temple architecture, the Lamp Tower. The concept of a pillar with lights on it as an offering to the deity is one of extreme antiquity, but seems to have been particularly developed at this period by the Marathas. The original concept may well have been suggested by the Islamic minarets, symbols of the religion against which the Marathas fought, but whatever the origin, the first occurrences in Goa are as pillars with a series of ledges concealing narrow troughs for containing oil. The wicks would rest on the ledges

46 The Shri Kamaxi temple at Shiroda

and when they were lit at festival times the pillar would become a column of light.

These pillars are in fact 'deepa stambha' or 'deepmala' as they are known locally, 'light columns', and as such are not unknown in other parts of Hindu India. The peculiarly Goan development was in the transformation of these pillars into major 'stambha' towers. Again the architectural style was purely European Baroque, and they frequently partnered the form of the dome. Usually octagonal, the towers have many storeys with windows on each face flanked by pilasters as in the drum of the domes, and in these windows lamps would be placed to convert them to veritable towers of light.

One possible origin for this transformation were the many piazza and wayside crosses which enliven the Goan landscape, many of which have quite complicated high pedestals, often octagonal and highly decorated. An extension of this, combined with the pillar concept might well have resulted in the stambha towers. Whatever the origin they are extremely impressive adjuncts to the major temples, and a uniquely Goan phenomenon. The Chittor towers in Rajasthan, although known as stambha towers, are in fact 'kirti' stambha or Victory towers, and have no real connection with the light towers.

The original temple of Mahalsa, now at Mardol near Ponda, was at Verna in Salcete district, and was apparently extremely beautiful and impressive. It is first mentioned in the governorship of Duarte de Menezes, 1522 to 1524, when one of 'Adil Shah's captains, with 5,000 men, attacked and laid siege to a group of Portuguese for two days who were in the temple 'which was like a fortress', and in 1567 Gomes Vaz wrote, 'At the entrance of the Temple of Verna there is a Chapel or tank with an arched roof similar to the Church of Our Lady of Divar, and having a portal of black stone. Truly, I have not seen such a fabulous one, even in Portugal.' When the images were finally destroyed at the request of Fr. Luis Goes, even he was so moved by the beauty of the temple that he wished to preserve it to house Our

Lady of Conception, Queen of the Angels. His request was rejected and the temple was destroyed, but not before the image of Mahalsa and a number of others had been removed to a place of safety.

At Mardol the temple was re-erected (*col. pl. 38*, pl. 47, plan 5) in the manner which had become traditional in Goa, and again this temple owes much to subsequent rebuildings. The carved wooden pillars which support the roof of the front hall are particularly beautiful, the intricacies of the carving belying the solidity of the wood. There are also a number of carvings which relate to the Shakti cult as well as a fine series of the ten avatars or incarnations of Vishnu. The goddess Mahalsa is a form of the goddess Lakshmi, the consort of Vishnu, and it is therefore not unusual to find carvings of Vishnu in her temple, and there is indeed a very rare series of eighteen of the twenty-four images of Vishnu, indicating the universal action of the god, in the temple of Mahalakshmi at Bandora in Ponda district.

A recent addition to the temple of Mahalsa is an enormous brass Garuda pillar which stands in front of the temple alongside the stambha tower. Like similar Garuda pillars in Nepal the pillar rests on the back of a turtle, which is the second avatar of Vishnu, and is surmounted by the Garuda, the sacred vehicle of Vishnu which is half-man half-eagle. The pillar in this position therefore represents the Axis Mundi, the sacred Mount Meru which is at the centre of the universe, but this particular version is also a deepa stambha, and is made up of a series of lamps forming a column. In Goa, at least on this occasion, there would therefore appear to be some confusion between the two forms of pillar, or else the light pillar must also be always regarded as a form of the cosmic pillar.

The temple of Manguesh, a beneficent aspect of Shiva, at Priol was founded in the sixteenth century to receive the stone idol from the original Manguesh temple at Cortalim in Salcete district. By 1566 one of the priests sent from the College of St Paul in Goa, was able to write back that 'the Hindus of Cortalim had already taken some of their deities to other places leaving the Temples deserted,' and in consequence a church was built on the site of the old temple.

The present temple at Priol (*col. pls. 39–40*, pls. 48–49, plan 6) is one of the most important in Goa and is the principal shrine of Shiva, in consequence it is extremely rich and is constantly growing. Again the nucleus of the temple possibly dates back to the eighteenth century or even earlier, but this has been much overlaid. There are many nineteenth century additions to the main shrine but these do not detract from its principal lines, and with all parts painted a gleaming white, it appears magnificent set against the rich groves of palm-trees which surround it.

Most of the temples in Goa conform to this style of architecture, with of course individual variations, but there are a few which have other derivations. The temple of Vitthala, an aspect of Vishnu, which was recently renovated by the Ranes of Sanquelim, is much more in the style of a North Indian temple. It has been very well rebuilt, and since the Ranes came from Rajasthan, it is only natural that they should have retained some of that architectural tradition. A number of the original carved wooden columns have been retained inside the new temple as museum exhibits, and there is also a magnificent wooden temple cart with an image of Hanuman which is housed nearby.

The Ranes still live in an old family house which is alongside the temple at Sanquelim, and it is interesting to compare houses built for some of the great Hindu

47 The Shri Mahalsa temple at Mardol

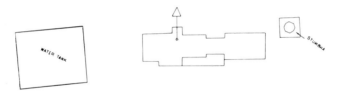

Plan 5 Shri Mahalsa temple

48 Shri Manguesh temple; entrance to the tank

49 Shri Manguesh temple; the great lamp tower with the tulasi vrindavana in front

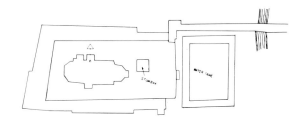

Plan 6 Shri Manguesh temple, Priol

50 A village tulasi vrindavan, the decorative pot in which
the sacred Hindu tulasi plant is grown and which is found
in every Hindu house

families with those previously discussed. As with so many large family houses this one has also been divided, and the long facade is neatly bisected by a salient block whose fortress-like appearance masks a change in level from the older, lower building to the slightly higher more formally planned section. The older part rests on massive stone columns, and the first floor living rooms contain superbly carved brackets and capitals, which are probably contemporaneous with the wooden columns preserved in the temple, and which blend perfectly with the comfortable, book-filled decor.

A completely different style of house is that of the Sinai-Kundaikers, originally built some two hundred and fifty years ago, even before Pombal had curbed the powers of the Inquisition. The house stands in the centre of a region famed for growing arica nuts, the basic constituent of Pan, which all Indians seem to chew, and this formed the foundation of the family fortunes.

The house has recently been given a welcoming porch, but prior to this it must have presented a much more fortress-like appearance. The facade of the low, two-storeyed house has small barred windows on the ground floor, and the windows on the upper floor are fitted with shutters. The front doors are made of metal and open into a small hall which is closed by another set of metal doors. Alongside each pair of doors are small holes drilled through the walls which were big enough for rifles to poke through and attack any intruders; particularly effective for any unwelcome guests who had managed to break through the first set of doors and were attacking the second set in the narrow confines of the hall. Obviously the eighteenth century in this part of Goa was not a place for taking chances.

Once inside, the house is grouped around a courtyard with a covered arcade on all four sides, off which open the main reception rooms. The main salon has some very fine examples of carved rosewood furniture, and among the family portraits which decorate the walls is the picture of one member of the family who was knighted by the Portuguese Crown for his services to Goa. In 1900 this salon was redecorated and the walls and ceiling were painted with a series of landscapes and allegorical scenes which was very unusual in Goa. The private apartments are grouped around a second courtyard which lies further back in the house. This again was an unusual practice but one which ensured that the family was able to lead a strict Hindu life in private while at the same time maintaining an open, landlord style life in the public rooms, where their hospitality was always legendary, a custom they still maintain.

Not far from the house is the village temple, a fine example of Hindu temple building and one undoubtedly built with funds from the Kundaiker family. The name of the village is Kundai, and the 'ker' ending is to signify that the family came from, or were the landlords of that particular village or area. This was a very common practice among Hindu families, as in Khandepar where the Khandeparker family live in a delightful courtyard house which was built in 1890 in which they also still continue to dispense traditional hospitality.

One Hindu house that also still maintains a major tradition of help and hospitality is the old Dempo house in Panjim which has now become almost a charitable institution. The Dempos are one of the older Hindu families in Goa, and, with considerable forethought, had moved their house from Old Goa to Panjim sometime in the seventeenth century. They were a great merchant family, but more important, they were Goud Saraswat Brahmins, members of the old nobility with a long aristocratic tradition, part of which has always consisted of charitable acts. Every day food has always been offered to the needy, and in particular to the students, for the Dempos have always supported education.

The family actually moved from the old house in 1914 and went to Santa Cruz, but one representative of the family has continued to visit the house daily to partake of food and to continue the old rituals. Food is still offered each day to the needy, although fewer avail themselves of this nowadays, nor of the possibility of staying in the house although a basic essential staff is still maintained. The house underwent major renovations some two hundred years ago, and is built around a central courtyard in the centre of which is the tulasi vrindavana (see pl. 50), the decorative pot in which the sacred Hindu plant grows, an essential feature of all Hindu houses.

Much of the house has been destroyed or swallowed up within government offices and even the prison, but the verandah alongside the courtyard still retains enough atmosphere to imagine some of the life of a Hindu family in the very middle of Portuguese Goa.

Not far away, opposite the Secretariat, is the Mamai Kamat House, also dating to the seventeenth century. This house is unusual in that it is still home to one of the great extended Hindu families comprising about one hundred people in nine groups. They still have a communal messing system which, amongst other things, requires a sack of rice each day. They still own a few shops around the house but the income from these has dwindled considerably over the years.

However, undoubtedly the grandest house in Goa is that of the Deshprabhu family in Pernem. The great nineteenth century facade conceals a complex of sixteen courtyards, the plinth of the house covering an area of twenty-eight hectares. The Drum Tower of the house is still used to announce the three services a day in the temple, while a gong is rung every hour to announce the time, particularly for the workers.

The present owners have created a very interesting museum within the first courtyard which contains many of the artifacts associated with such a splendid household. Given the title of Viscount by the Portuguese, they lived as befitted great landowning aristocrats and the solid silver palanquins in which they were carried to the temple as children are only the highlights of this magnificent collection. The house and its collection represent one of the highlights of the Hindu contribution to the multi-faceted Goan kaleidoscope.

GOA TODAY

Long beaches of golden sands fringed with waving palm trees; brilliant green paddy fields framing a gleaming white church; glistening mounds of silver fish amid the nets on the beach at dawn; superbly cooked meals abounding in masses of the most delectable shellfish; meandering conversations about every aspect of life and death, punctuated by copious draughts of feni; a guitarist, hauntingly singing Portuguese songs while our boat wandered through the inland waterways; the mad, exuberant crowd dancing through the streets during Carnival. All of these and many more are the memories which Goa evokes.

The great churches, the forts, the temples and palatial mansions, are all there as backdrops to an intensely moving relationship which everyone seems to develop the moment they encounter Goa. In this sun-drenched atmosphere, stimulated by two thousand years of colourfully embroidered history which represents the whole sub-continent in a microcosm, a way of life has been evolved which has a great deal to offer even the most casual visitor. And this is emphasised by the marvellous way the Goans welcome you into their lives and homes to take part in that way of life.

Even in the magnificent series of superb hotels which now adorn the beaches of Goa like a string of twentieth century palaces the visitor is made to feel welcome and is shown varied facets of this way of life. And everywhere the vibrant colours of the bougainvillea cascade down the sides of houses and hotels, adding a strident note to the thick lush green foliage from which the buildings rise.

Traditionally the Goan economy has been based on a healthy mixture of the land and the sea. Agriculture and fishing have supplied the needs of the people abundantly, the high protein content of the fish making the various sea-food curries an extremely healthy diet. Additionally the sea has also brought trade and it was as a great trading port that Goa made its presence known in history, both before and after the arrival of the Portuguese. Without her magnificent anchorages Goa would be simply another coastal strip on the immensity of India.

The Zuari and the Mandovi created the Goa that can be seen today and always, while wandering around the streets of Panjim, one is conscious that this is really a port city. The old, narrow streets with their tavernas leading down to the river, particularly in the area of Fontainhas behind the main Post Office, all indicate the life of a sea trading community, even if the main port has now shifted to Vasco on the Zuari. Goa was, and still is the port which fed so much of southern India with a wealth of products, although her supreme position was long ago taken by Bombay, and it was the wealth from the trade which built the marvellous monuments which still remain.

This is one of the points which must be remembered when looking at the magnificent churches which stand in splendid isolation in Old Goa. When Old Goa and the churches were alive they were pulsing with the life of a sea port. The houses crowded up to the churches and convents in a maze of streets through which the merchant princes picked their way amid a milling throng. Its opulence dazzled all visitors so that the saying arose, 'who has seen Goa need not see Lisbon,' and still the wealth flowed in from all the areas of the far-flung Portuguese empire. The triumphal entries of the victorious viceroys were pagan in their splendour with flowers thrown down in front of the chariots and horses from the storeyed balconies of the seigneurial houses.

Wandering through the lush green parks which nowadays surround the few remaining churches it is difficult to picture the life which once pulsated all around but it is certainly worthwhile making the effort to clothe this green nudity with a little imagination. One of the places where this is slightly easier is down by the river, past the Arch of the Viceroys. Some remnants of the massive walls which once girded the city can still be seen and, as other river boats discharge a rather more mundane cargo, it is tempting to picture the merchant ships with their opulent contents, tying up at the same wharf and presenting themselves at the Customs House. This lay to the left of the road, outside the walls, and is now a grove of palm trees, but the wealth of broken pottery attests to its former state.

From this point the visitors followed the road under the arch and were then engulfed in the hubbub of the streets of the capital. At this stage modern imagination tends to break down since nothing can be seen but empty roads, trees and lots of greenery, but perhaps for a brief moment some inkling of the former magnificent life may have been glimpsed. Now Old Goa has lost this dramatic aspect, along with the cholera and the malaria which eventually caused its disintegration, only the churches survive as relics of former splendour.

Panjim also has lost some of its more frenetic side with the transfer of the main port, but the fish market is still there, screaming with life every day as the buyers and sellers haggle over the prices. It also springs to life with the arrival and departure of the daily boat from Bombay bringing all types of people to enjoy the beauties of Goa, or bidding them a fond, perhaps tearful farewell.

Although most tourists take the forty-five minutes flight from Bombay, landing near Vasco and then driving to their respective hotels, those with more time, or perhaps less money, or simply with a more leisurely approach to life, tend to take the boat and spend about twenty hours on the journey. During the high season all the cabins are booked months in advance, mainly by Goan families returning home for the holidays, which leaves the deck as the next best thing. This is usually filled with the more uninhibited younger crowd who have been coming to Goa since the early 60s and who still represent the majority of Western tourists in the territory. Their arrivals and departures add a welcome colourful note of bustle and disorder to Panjim's waterfront which, momentarily, feels itself rejuvenated. After a few hectic moments as the travellers sort themselves out before heading for the beaches where they will live, the waterfront returns to its habitual, more somnolent lifestyle, the locals probably going into one of the nearby bars to relax after their exertions.

Mention of the bars brings one inevitably to a discussion of feni, the local Goan drink which is almost impossible to discover outside Goa because the Goans, very sensibly, drink it all themselves. There are two kinds of feni, palm and cashew, the one is distilled from palm toddy and is the milder version to which visitors are normally introduced whereas cashew feni is for the more regular topers. This is made by first crushing the cashew apple, the red fruit which forms immediately above the cashew nut. The resultant liquid is then distilled and the result is pure nectar. Usually drunk with a number of mixes to make a long drink, it is occasionally possible to obtain some eighteen year old feni which can be most favourably compared with many better known liqueurs and makes a splendid digestive drink. To appreciate the true flavour of Fontainhas an early evening glass at Joseph's Bar followed by a well-cooked dinner in one of the many neighbourhood hotels or restaurants will present the balconied houses and little streets at their magical best.

Shops and offices in Panjim are often behind pillared arcades, particularly in the centre of the town, which means that it possible to shop and stroll while missing the heat of the sun. After the midday heat is over people move around more freely, crossing the two central squares for example, either to admire the gardens in the one or to see the Albuquerque memorial (pl. 51) in the other. It is also possible to stroll along the esplanade which lines the river bank, looking at the boats or simply looking at the other people strolling, however so much exercise soon gives rise to a thirst which requires quenching in one of the cafes or in the bar of the Mandovi hotel which has long been the place to meet friends and admire the view of the river. During Carnival it provides a perfect view of the procession, the dancers being encouraged by frequent shouts from friends leaning out of various windows.

For those people who like a little more exercise a westward continuation of the esplanade meets the Miramar beach, another rendezvous for an evening stroll, however an expedition to Dona Paula is best done by taxi. This headland looks across the Zuari to Vasco da Gama and ferries, inevitably overcrowded, ply between the two points, although this is not the only reason for going there. The point is supposedly named after a viceroy's daughter who, legend has it, fell in love with a fisherman whom she could not marry and so jumped into the sea from the cliffs. The pavilion which stands precariously on the edge of the cliff is a perfect place to watch the sunset across the dark waters of the Arabian Sea. The secluded beach nearby has some excellent tourist accommodation and the restaurant serves very good meals, specialising in the usual superb seafood.

The buildings at Dona Paula have been well-designed and, while not attempting to blend in with the landscape, are attractive as are the majority of very new buildings, particularly those associated with tourism, which have appeared recently. Unfortunately there is a sad legacy from the early sixties. In the initial rush to cope with the problems of a growing tourist market, which was immediately apparent after the incorporation of Goa into India in 1961, a number of tourist buildings were erected which will, hopefully, be rendered obsolete in the near future and removed or replaced. The creation of a Planning Department with powers to oversee all new buildings is a very healthy sign and the phrase, 'nothing higher than a palm-tree', should become an inspiring slogan.

At the same time a vocabulary of traditional architecture is being created taking the principle elements which constitute the Goan houses and using them in any new buildings. Such ideas as Mangalore tiled roofs, the use of porches and balconies, particularly incorporating the balcão type seats so conducive of gossip, the idea of the courtyard house and even, occasionally, the use of oyster shells instead of glass for windows. Above all the use of colours which do not clash with the rest of the buildings. Perhaps the two colours most associated with Goa are ochre and white, although obviously many others have also been used, the important point, however, is to avoid colours that have no relationship with buildings around them, such as the unfortunate 'corporation green' which has been so liberally daubed over much of the English countryside.

51 The monument to Afonso de Albuquerque in the main square in Panjim

With a few exceptions the major new hotels which have been built in the past few years have taken into account the local architectural style and have blended sensitively into the landscape. An outstanding example of this is the Fort Aguada hotel, which forms part of the Taj Group. Set within the confines of the old Portuguese fort, it has been landscaped back into the hill and does not in any way obtrude upon the skyline. The main block is grouped around a terrace with a swimming pool, while behind rise a series of individual cottages set in an amazing garden which has completely reclothed the headland in a mass of luxuriant foliage so that the whole seems like a well-tended village rather than an hotel.

The main hotel has now been joined by the Taj Holiday Village which is situated on the beach itself and consists of a series of cottages and villas modelled on original Goan buildings. Apparently the architects studied over three hundred houses in order to achieve authenticity and the buildings which they have created conform perfectly to the Goan architectural vocabulary. The presence of this whole complex at the southern end of Calangute beach has created a very luxurious ambience in which the most international traveller will find few things to fault. However, further to the north along the beach, the atmosphere changes completely and in the area of Calangute itself used to be found the principle centre of the psychedelic movement. The beach itself is eleven kilometres long and has always managed to contain both types of traveller with absolute equanimity. Nowadays the majority of the more uninhibited younger set have moved to the beaches further north but there is still a sufficiently large group to provide a friendly foil to the travellers at the other end of the beach.

Part of the magic of Goa consists in this ability to mix different groups and produce a happy amalgam and, since both groups seem to enjoy walking, there is a very friendly intermingling along the beach. This can be seen particularly in the early morning when the fishermen are hauling in their nets. One may come to photograph and the other to buy but at that hour of the morning everybody meets at the same level and there's really not much distinction between bathing-suits.

Another very successful addition to the Goan scene is the Welcomgroup hotel called Cidade-de-Goa which is on a beach just to the east of Dona Paula. The concept behind the hotel was to create a Portuguese village along the beach, complete with main street, central square and several piazzas, as well as a splendid wide flight of steps leading down to the beach with a fantastic view across palm trees to the sea. Staircases lead up and down to the various rooms which are arranged as though they were different houses while the piazzas form the bars and main congregational areas. Seen from the beach it looks like a small hill town and blends in perfectly with the landscape.

The imaginative approach to hotel design is an encouraging sign and, as other major hotel chains realise the potential of Goa as a major tourist destination, it is to be hoped that they will also follow this initiative and create something which is in keeping with the Goan lifestyle. An additional incentive will surely be the attitude of the travellers themselves who will undoubtedly prefer hotels which provide some measure of local ambience and at least make a gesture of acknowledging the existence of the growing ecological and conservationist movements in the world today.

This attitude should not of course be restricted to the creation of the major hotels but can equally well be applied to much smaller units. The Baia do Sol Hotel at Baga beach just north of Calangute is an example of sensitive design on a smaller scale, blending in successfully among the palm trees of one of the most attractive of the northern beaches. The somewhat uncompromising architectural stand of the great Oberoi hotel at Bogmalo beach is being softened by extensive planting and a tendency to concentrate on the interiors and the wide range of sea sports which the hotel offers along its superb private beach.

One other interesting result of the ecological movement has been the creation of game sanctuaries within Goa. At the moment there are three of these, a small one at Bondla in the centre of Goa, the largest at Molem in the east, and a third, still largely undeveloped in the south at Cotigao. The 80 square kilometres at Bondla are more in the nature of a zoo with considerable facilities for education which certainly attracts the local schoolchildren. There is also a well-landscaped garden as well as a wild garden and a deer park and a series of tourist cottages in the centre near the restaurant.

The Baghwan Mahaveer Sanctuary at Molem is very different and more in the nature of a sanctuary. Its 240 square kilometres contain a magnificent herd of Indian bison as well as elephants, leopard, deer and other wild animals in addition to an abundant bird life. So far it is in the early stages and still needs considerable planning before it will become a major tourist attraction but, at the moment, it is possible to enjoy a pleasant bird-watching walk without too many distractions. So far the southern sanctuary has not been developed at all and is purely acting as a sanctuary for the animals in its vicinity.

However, despite the various other attractions it is the beaches for which Goa is justifiably famous and which merit a complete section to themselves. Miles of

52 Bridge in the centre of Panjim

53 A road in Altinho leading to the Patriarchal Palace

54 The Patriarchal Palace in Altinho, built in the late nineteenth century

55 A view over Panjim from Altinho showing a new Hindu temple

white or golden sand leading into a gentle, warm sea, with swaying palms fringing the landward side, they are unsurpassed in this part of the world, the main problem being to decide which one to choose. Mention has already been made of the beach at Calangute which has always been described as the 'Queen' of Goa's beaches. This is probably because of the life of which it was the centre during the 60s and 70s, much of which has now quietened down considerably during the more restricted 80s, but the beauty of the beach still remains. It may have fewer palm trees than others and the decline into the sea is perhaps less gentle but eleven kilometres of golden sand is still a very good beach. Baga, just to the north, is less crowded and still clings to its quiet charm with the additional advantage that it is only a couple of kilometres walk along the beach to join in the life of Calangute if so desired.

At the end of the 70s, when Calangute had apparently been so totally over-exposed that it no longer had any attractions, everyone moved to Anjuna still further to the north and many of them still remain there to this day. It is still a place of few inhibitions and consequently retains its popularity among one group of travellers. Just to the north of Anjuna is Chapora, still one of the most beautiful and interesting parts of Goa. The area is dominated by a headland on which the fort is built and around which the village nestles under a canopy of dense coconut palms. This is the area to which most of the Westerners flock, usually staying in houses in the village, although a new series of cottages, called the Vagator Beach Resort, now caters for a more affluent type of traveller who can, at the same time, enjoy all the other advantages of the area, including the small, sandy coves around the headland which make a change from the main beach.

The most northerly point of Goa is marked by Teracol fort and beach, beautifully situated at the confluence of the river and the sea. The fort has now been converted into a tourist hotel with very simple accommodation but the utter peace and tranquillity are worth the journey and any marginal discomfort.

Because of hotel development and the main tourist movement attention has largely been concentrated on the northern beaches but in the south of Goa are some of the most beautiful beaches to be found anywhere. Forty kilometres of unspoilt, clean white sand, fringed with palm trees and gently sloping into the sea make Colva beach unique. It has been described as 'a touch of Paradise', and it is easy to understand why a number of leading hoteliers are seriously considering expanding their operations into this area. Around Colva itself the fishermen land their catch and also dry the fish which does tend to impart a fishy flavour to the atmosphere at this point, but a few minutes walk leads to total solitude. So far there are only a few tourist cottages around a good seafood restaurant. These have been well designed and hopefully, any future development of the area would follow the imaginative lines which other hotels have chosen and avoid the usual concrete blocks which have disfigured so many of the world's best beaches.

Beyond Colva beach, beyond Cabo de Rama, the most southerly of the forts of Goa, there is finally the beach of Palolem for those people who are really wanting to get away from it all. Almost a secret beach, it is usually practically completely deserted and has a backdrop of the lower ranges of the Western Ghats leading down to the sea.

From Teracol in the north to Palolem in the south Goa has fantastic beaches to suit all tastes with similar varying styles of accommodation on them. Over the past twenty-five years they have attracted a wide variety of travellers, all of whom have fallen beneath their spell and have continued to return time and again. As the tourist infrastructure grows, so they have become available to an even wider range of travellers who will also, hopefully, want to explore beyond the beaches and to find out more about the rest of Goa. Because however beautiful the beach and the hotel, this is only a fraction of what Goa has to offer and the traveller should certainly see the Goan life in the villages.

The vast majority of people still live in the villages which dot the landscape, usually clustered protectively around a white-painted church. Here can be seen the bustling markets, all noise, scents and smells; a strange mixture of fish and flowers which is peculiarly Goan. The buxom, garrulous fish wives, who were up at dawn haggling shrilly with fishermen on the beach as they pulled in their nets, are now smilingly enticing people to buy their fish, using quite different tones from the earlier raucous cries. Wonderful fresh fruits are displayed in a riot of colour and the bargaining is loud and vociferous. Fortunately there is always a bar next door where everyone can have a beer or a feni and relax.

In Goa there is always a bar next door, and there is always time to stop for a drink and a chat. Conversation is one of the living arts of Goa, all house porches have seats built into them so that people can sit and watch the world go by and discuss it all in great detail, preferably while it is all still happening. The uncharitable would call this gossiping, but to the Goan it is the very breath of life, and nothing helps the conversation flow as much as a glass of feni, or possibly two!

The villages also contain really beautiful examples of the Goan house style, most of them painted white with colourful doors and windows, and flowers everywhere. Many of them are also grouped around some big house, which, while not perhaps in the same class as some of the mansions already discussed, is still of considerable architectural value. Some of these have been deserted because the families have either emigrated or can no longer maintain them, but even in decay, they have a timeless quality which comes from original good breeding and fine lines. Some of course are still the homes of the local landlord, who is very likely to receive guests wearing elegant striped pyjamas. This is to make sure that everyone realises that he doesn't have to work and is a member of the leisured classes. Goa still enjoys a considerable class differential, although this is rapidly changing under the exigencies of modern living.

The church is still however the centre point of Goan life in the Old Conquests, particularly in the villages, and the local priest exercises an important and much respected role in the community. He is the local counsellor and is called in to advise on all occasions, even those which may have little to do with his spiritual calling, but of course, he comes into his own on the great occasions such as weddings and the numerous festivals which enliven the calendar. Weddings can be either simple village affairs or much grander occasions which call for, not merely a great display at the church, but also enormous festivities afterwards where the bride and groom soon fade into the background as the festival spirit quickly envelops everyone else. Such receptions either take place in one or other of the big houses, or, if the ceremony is being conducted in Panjim, it might he held in one of the gracious clubs, such as the Club Nacional, which also play such an important role in organising the greatest event of the Goan social calendar, the annual Carnival.

Festivals, either Christian or Hindu, occupy an important place in the Goan year, and they are all celebrated with considerable gusto. Every parish has the feast of its local saint, but certain saints seem to be venerated all over Goa, or else in special places which equally attract all Goans. The Feast of the Three Kings is

56 The lobby of the Fort Aguada hotel

57 One of the specially designed cottages in the Taj Village hotel

celebrated on 6 January in Cuelim in South Goa and also with a great fair at Reis
Magos near Fort Aguada. The fort at Reis Magos is one of the oldest, and the church
was the first to be erected in North Goa and has many viceregal associations.

In Goa Velha St Andrew's church is the proud possessor of twenty-six statues
of saints which are brought out in procession on the Monday following the fifth
Sunday in Lent. Rome is the only other place in the world which has a similar
procession, and when the Goan one was started in the seventeenth century it
featured sixty-five statues. As the procession moves through the streets, people line
up to run under the palanquins on which each statue is carried as a way of winning
the saint's blessing. This feast is also accompanied by the inevitable fair at which
hand fans are sold as a regional speciality.

One of the biggest fairs is held at Mapuca on the nearest Sunday sixteen days
after Easter on the occasion of a feast which is jointly celebrated by Hindus and
Christians. This is that of Our Lady of Miracles, who is also venerated by Hindus as
Lairaya, the goddess of the Sirigaum Temple. Mapuca is the centre for the Friday
market to which all Goans come, and this feast is simply an enormous extension of
the usual market, but one which has also been given religious overtones.

The feast of St Anthony on 13 June is associated with the coming of the rains
which have always been crucial for the life of the farmers, and the songs which are
sung on this occasion are all along the theme of asking St Anthony to send rain. If
for some reason the rains don't come on the 13th there is still another feast on the
24 June, a traditional second resort for a late monsoon. The Feast of St John the
Baptist is usually a thanksgiving for the rains, and mainly consists of groups of
young men singing their way around the village requesting contributions of feni.
Naturally things tend to get slightly out of hand, and as the evening wears on the
Feast gets celebrated by the young men jumping into the wells. These are situated
in almost every courtyard, so no one has very far to go, and the water level is usually
fairly high so that there is little danger. The custom is fairly widespread, but it can
be seen very successfully at Calangute.

The monsoon is obviously one of the high points of the year, and there are a
number of water associated festivals at this time, apart from which there is not
much else to do when it's raining. One of these is naturally that of St Peter, the
patron saint of fishermen, which falls on 29 June. The festival takes place near Fort
Aguada where three local fishing villages lash a number of boats together to form a
stage, and then re-enact a sort of pageant on this stage as it floats majestically down
the river. Another of these monsoon festivals is the Feast of St Lawrence on 10
August, at the end of the rainy season. The church of St Lawrence was built in 1630
and is a superb white edifice on the north bank of the Mandovi near its mouth. In
Goa St Lawrence is the patron saint of sailors, and the feast signals the opening of
the sandbars which have built up in the Mandovi during the monsoon and
obstructed shipping. For some inexplicable reason they usually do break up on this
day and the boats are able to sail out the next day.

Novidade is the great Harvest Festival of Goa and is celebrated on 21 August
each year. The first paddy is cut, and offerings are made to the priests, and on 24
August some more rice is carried to the Cathedral at Old Goa, and then to the
Governor and Archbishop. There is also a dramatic re-enactment of the battle
between Albuquerque and the 'Adil Shah's soldiers which used to take place in

front of the Governor's palace, but now takes place more privately on the lawns of the Lieutenant Governor's palace.

The Hindus of Goa, as all over India, celebrate the birth of Lord Krishna in late August with bathing in the river Mandovi off Diwadi island, a spectacle which the Inquisition frowned on considerably in former times, and also have a major procession and firecrackers to celebrate Divali, the New year, which occurs around the end of October. Both religions however seem to celebrate Easter and Christmas in one way or another, and everyone possible goes mad at Carnival.

For weeks beforehand people are preparing costumes, and having endless meetings trying to decide on themes and float designs for the great day, all of which is greatly helped along by copious draughts of beer and feni. As the day draws near rehearsals begin, and the various groups begin to practise dance steps to an appropriate record, although the record player seems to have a mind of its own and keeps breaking down. Tension mounts, and last minute costumes are quickly made, and fitted, in furtive backstage rooms. The atmosphere is full of secrets, and the rivalry between certain groups is obviously well-established, although everything is done in the spirit of Carnival.

The great day dawns, and people begin to gather at the rendezvous points, so that by late afternoon the various processions are ready to move off and gather near the Secretariat where the main procession route begins. The crowds are thick, the music boisterous from twenty different groups, some of which are a hundred strong and all dressed in wild colours. The parade begins and dances and twists its way through the streets of Panjim, until finally it is over for another year. Somebody has won the prize, but nobody really minds who, as the dancers reel back to their homes to prepare for the dance in the evening.

For four days Goa sleeps during the day so that it can dance all night. Each of the big clubs arranges a dance for one of the nights, and traffic and everything else must make way for this. The Vasco da Gama Club has a dance in the central gardens, while the Club Nacional manages to get the entire road closed in front of their clubhouse and traffic is quite simply diverted, along with the rest of Goa. After four days of this Goans reel back to work, and the austerities of Lent begin, but by then nobody really minds, and there is always next year to start planning for.

The sense of drama which is naturally inherent in Carnival finds its expression in other ways during the rest of the year. Well known for a rich tradition of theatrical performances, over a thousand shows are reportedly staged in Goa annually, the vast majority of which are produced by amateurs during festival occasions. These have received considerable support from Goa's Kala Academy, now housed in splendid modern quarters along the Miramar road, which has arranged a series of annual drama contests.

These contests have been divided into three classes, one in Marathi and two in Konkani and, not only have the number of contestants steadily increased each year, but also the quality has risen. The vast majority of the plays performed in Goa are Marathi, generally written by playwrights from Maharashtra, but an increasing number of Konkani plays are being produced, written by Goans. Considering that there was really no written Konkani literature until the seventeenth century, it augurs well for the literary development of the language that such developments are taking place.

58 The *Flor da Rosa*, an engaging way of visiting the backwaters of Goa

59 The Oberoi hotel at Bogmalo beach

60 The Welcomgroup's Cidade de Goa hotel

61 One of the ferries which carries everything across the various rivers in the territory

62 The elegant facade of one of the larger village houses which has now been abandoned

63 Boats and palm trees on a Goan river

With all of these festivals Goa has also managed to develop an excellent cuisine which owes something to India, something to Portugal, and a great deal to the excellent raw materials which are so abundantly provided by nature. Chicken, pork, duck, mutton, and of course suckling pig, are ingredients which abound and complement the rich variety of fish of all kinds which fill the rivers and the nearby sea, so that the Goan menu is anything but restricted. Shellfish in particular is a Goan speciality, and crabs of all sizes, lobsters, and magnificent tiger prawns, big enough to form a meal in themselves, are practically staple fare. Rice is the most general accompaniment, but other vegetables are available, and indeed anything will grow in the rich soil.

Like all Indians, Goans have a sweet tooth, and from a very limited range of ingredients have managed to produce an incredible variety of desserts and special sweet concoctions which are the highlights of all festivals, and especially Christmas. Using coconuts, rice, semolina, eggs and flour, all mixed with various spices and essences, they create a list of sweet delicacies, all the more astounding in that each is so different. The names themselves are redolent of hidden delights: Bibinca, Kulkuls, Teias de Aranha, Bolinhas, Bolo Gostoso and Sans Rival and are worthy of the hours, sometimes days spent preparing them.

Most of these delicacies are made at home and are the pride of the family kitchen, with a certain amount of friendly rivalry existing between families. At all of these feasts parcels of a particular speciality will be sent to different houses each of which reciprocates with the pride of their own kitchens. The children are the natural messengers for this exchange and the equally happy recipients of samples at every destination although the serious moment is only reached when each cook tastes her rival's specialities. A number of hotels and restaurants also serve a wide variety of the seemingly inexhaustible Goan cuisine in addition to the more usual international menu, but when it comes to preparing one of the special sweets as a dessert offering, there is usually a nearby Goan lady, whose Bibinca is locally famous, who provides a fresh supply each day.

Thus, in so many ways, the older Goan customs and skills are being assimilated into the present and this is an assimilation which can only be advantageous to both sides. Change is inevitable and natural but should always proceed out of the past rather than attempting to reject it. At the moment, with very few exceptions, this amalgam of old and new is working very successfully in Goa and should be both continued and developed. Despite attempts to industrialise, modernise and generally standardise, Goa remains maddeningly, delightfully different as are so many of the other states in India. India herself is a total world, containing all possible varieties of people and places, so that the jewel which is Goa, simply adds yet another facet to the whole which in turn benefits by such an addition.

From the lush green countryside, densely planted with rice, pineapples and bananas and fringed with palms, through the happy, untidy villages, to the endless sweeping golden beaches, Goa is a richly warm experience. Two thousand years of history have left strange and magnificent remains on her shore but, most of all, have created a warm and friendly people who are the greatest treasure in Goa – and to whom this book is dedicated.

NOTES FOR THE TRAVELLER

General

Goa has an area of 3,702 sq km. The altitude ranges from sea-level to 1,022 metres. The population is just over 1 million. Administratively Goa is split into 11 talukas.

Tourist information can be obtained from the Government of India Tourist Office, Communidada Building, Church Square, Panjim (tel: 3412).

Routes

AIR TRAVEL

Goa's main airport facilities are at Dabolim, 29 km from Panjim. It is served at the time of publication by Air India, Vayudoot and Indian Airlines, who run an airport bus between their Panjim offices and Dabolim. There are connections to Bangalore, Bombay, Delhi, Cochin, Hyderabad and to other major Indian cities, and to Kuwait via Bombay.

Since Goa is becoming an increasingly popular destination for Europeans, there may be direct charter flights available to Goa from various European cities. It is advisable to consult your travel agent for information concerning particular flights.

RAIL TRAVEL

Margao is at present the most convenient station for Panjim. There are various express connections to major cities, including Bangalore, Bombay and Delhi.

One of the most romantic ways to tour India is by rail. Indian railways hark back to the grand old days of steam when railways were the only effective means of travel and were enhanced by a flexibility and spontaneity no longer extant in the West. There are hard-seated 2nd class compartments available or more comfortable 1st class tourist compartments. At the time of publication an Indrail pass for extended travel can be obtained from Indian railways.

BUS TRAVEL

There are many and varied connections to major towns in the area and further afield, including Bangalore, Belgaum, Bombay, Hubli, Karwar, Mangalore, Miraj, Mysore, Poona, Ratnagiri and Vengurla. It is best to enquire locally since companies offer various services and differing standards of transport.

ROAD TRAVEL

National Highways 4A, 17 and 17A connect with nearby towns and states. The major cities are linked by road at the following approximate distances and directions from Goa: Ahmedabad – 1138 km north; Aurangabad – 699 km northeast; Bangalore – 592 km southeast; Bombay – 594 km north; Madras – 923 km southeast; Poona – 473 km north.

SEA TRAVEL

A delightful and exotic way to complete the journey from Goa to Bombay or vice versa, without the problems of overland transport. Since it is popular amongst Goan families, it may be as well to book early for the high season.

There are daily sailings operated by the Shipping Corporation of India Ltd between Bombay and Panjim, except Tuesday from Bombay and Wednesday from Panjim. All sailings are suspended in the monsoon season or in rough weather. At present the sailing time is around 20 hours. Cabin and deck classes are available. Bookings can be made in Panjim at V S Dempo and Co. (tel: 3842) opposite the steamer jetty and New Ferry Wharf, Mallet Bunder, Bombay (tel: 864071).

LOCAL TRANSPORT

Journeys can be made by coach, tourist taxi, yellow-top taxi, motorcycle, flat-bottom ferry or launch.

Luxury coaches and air-conditioned or non-air-conditioned tourist taxis are bookable for short single trips or for extended times of several days from the Travel Division of the Goa Tourism Development Corporation, Panjim.

Yellow-top taxi and auto-rickshaws are charged by meter or arrangement with the driver before the journey, the latter being strongly advised.

Motorcycles are available for hire.

Ferries are used at various places to cross unbridged rivers; a small launch trip through the extensive waterways is perhaps one of the most delightful ways to experience Goa.

TOUR COMPANIES

Many tour companies now offer trips to Goa. Some of these feature Goa as a direct destination, with flights via Bombay, whilst other companies more frequently offer Goa as part of a southern India tour or as a three or four day optional extension to a regional tour of India.

The all-in tours generally include the major cities of the area, such as Bombay, Mysore, Bangalore and Cochin, as well as visits to locations of architectural and historic importance like the Vijayanagan capital of Hampi and the temples of Aihole and Pattadakal. Other popular tour destinations include wildlife reserves such as Mudumalai and Periyar and visits to the Nilgiri Hill country. Some of these tours are accompanied by expert guides and lecturers. A few tour companies are also willing to book reservations for itineraries prepared by travellers themselves if reasonable notification is given.

Some companies offer railway tours with accommodation en train or reserved for you at convenient stopping points.

There are a number of major US and European tour companies operating to the area. Companies to consult in the UK include: Abercrombie and Kent, Cox and Kings, Inspirations East Limited, Intasun, Page and Moy, Swan Hellenic Tours, Thomas Cook. Condor, based in West Germany, are one of the main companies operating from Europe.

EXCURSIONS

There are a variety of organised tours available to places of interest. Common groupings or suggestions at present include:

North Goa – Mayem Lake, Anjuna Beach and temples
South Goa – Panjim, Old Goa, Marmagao beach
Beaches – Calangute, Anjuna, Vagator
Religious buildings – Old Goa, including Bom Jesus and the See Cathedral, and the Ponda area, including the temples of Shri Manguesh, Shri Mahalsa, Shri Ramnath, Shri Shantadurga
Bondla wildlife sanctuary
Teracol fort
Tambdi Surla
River cruises by launch

Staying there

HOTELS

Tourists are advised to book well in advance. The following is not an exhaustive list and prices, star rating and facilities may well fluctuate:

5-STAR
Fort Aguada Beach Resort, Sinquerim
Taj Holiday Village, Sinquerim
Welcomgroup Cidade de Goa, Dona Paula
Oberoi, Bogmalo Beach
Majorda Beach Resort

3-STAR
Fidalgo, Panjim
Mandovi, Panjim
Keni's, Panjim

2-STAR
La Paz, Vasco da Gama
Zuari, Vasco da Gama
Noah's Ark Bamboo, Verem
Baia do Sol, Baga Beach

1-STAR
Hotel Solmar, Miramar Beach

There are a considerable number of hotels in Panjim, Margao, Vasco, Colva, Calangute, Benaulim, Vagator and Anjuna with relatively low-cost room rent. The cost at the present time is around Rs 120, or less, per night.

Other types of accommodation provided by the Directorate of Tourism include:
Teracol Fort Tourist Rest House
Mayem Lake Resort, Bicholim taluka
Tourist Resort, Molem, Sanguem
Youth Hostel, Miramar

FOOD
Goa is famous for its fish and shellfish, notably crabs, lobsters and tiger prawns. It also offers a wide variety of meat and poultry, including chicken, duck, mutton and pork. There is of course an ongoing tradition of vegetarian food. Rice is the main accompaniment. Goan desserts are especially delightful, many homemade, based on coconuts, rice, semolina, eggs and flour, with a variety of spices.

DRAMA
A large variety of local drama presentations, many supported by the Kala Academy and performed during festival occasions, occur in Goa. The Kala Academy itself arranges a series of annual drama contests for Marathi and Konkani plays.

CARNIVAL
Occurs during some 4 days of February or March preceding Lent. In Panjim there are street parades, floats, and dancing through the evenings and nights.

HINDU FESTIVALS
Major local Hindu festivals include:
Birth of Lord Krishna, late August – mass bathing in the river Mandovi off Diwadi Island
Divali, end of October – the Hindu New Year, celebrated with a major procession and fireworks

CHRISTIAN FESTIVALS
Major local Christian festivals include:
Feast of the Three Kings – celebrated on 6 January in Cuelim, Chandler and with a fair at Reis Magos near Fort Aguada.
Monday after the 5th Sunday in Lent – Procession, originating in the 17th century, of 26 statues of saints from the Church of St Andrew's in Goa Velha, the only procession of its kind outside Rome. Accompanied by a large fair where hand fans, a regional speciality, are sold.
Feast of Our Lady of Miracles (celebrated also by Hindus in honour of the goddess Lairaya), nearest Sunday 16 days after Easter – huge fair and market held in Mapuca.
Feast of St Anthony, 13 June – songs in honour of St Anthony and requesting the gift of rain.
Feast of St John the Baptist, 24 June – thanksgiving for rains, mostly at Calangute.

Young men tour the area singing for gifts of feni and jumping into wells!

Festival of St Peter, 29 June – Fort Aguada. Village boats are lashed together and a stage erected upon them. A pageant is re-enacted as the boats float down the river.

Feast of St Lawrence, 10 August – celebrates the opening of the sandbars in the Mandovi river.

Harvest Festival of Novidade, 21 and 24 August – first sheaves of rice crop offered to priests on 21st and then others cut and offered to the Governor, the Archbishop and placed in the Cathedral at Old Goa on the 24th. The festival includes a re-enactment on the lawns of the Lieutenant Governor's palace of a battle between Albuquerque and the 'Adil Shah.

SPORTS

There are a variety of sports offered to the tourist at various places in Goa, with many centred on clubs in Panjim, including: yachting, aqua sports, tennis, hiking and trekking. Some hotels and beach resort complexes offer their own sporting facilities; for example, the Fort Aguada Beach Resort provides fishing for salmon and mackerel, clay pigeon shooting and a general sports and fitness complex. There is, of course, plenty of opportunity to swim in hotel pools and the sea!

SEASONAL ADVICE

Although Goa's climate has all-year-round appeal, it is perhaps best for those not used to tropical climates and the monsoon to avoid the monsoon months of June to September.

Many tour companies operate a season of October to April, with November to February reckoned the most temperate (see CLIMATE). If travel further south to Madras, etc. is contemplated then January to April offers the clearest weather.

Climate demands clothing of cottons, unless trips to high inland areas like Ooty in the Nilgiri Hills are contemplated, where it may be advisable to take a sweater.

Visas are necessary for UK travellers to India – to be obtained before departure from the UK. Holders of non-UK passports may need visa/entry permits. Some travel companies are prepared to obtain visas, with a service charge, if application is made at least one month before departure.

Vaccinations are recommended by appropriate health authorities. Remember to book vaccinations well in advance of departure.

CLIMATE

Temperatures for January in Goa are between 20°C to 31°C and in April 25°C to 33°C. Rainfall averages 18 mm in January and 25 mm in April.

June to September is the monsoon season in Goa and rainfall can be exceptionally heavy.

Temperature and rainfall guide for months most favoured by tourists:

	Max-Min Temp °C	Average Rainfall mm		Max-Min Temp °C	Average Rainfall mm
Jan	20-31	18	Oct	23-31	23
Feb	20-32	20	Nov	22-33	23
Mar	23-32	23	Dec	21-33	20
Apr	25-33	25			

Places to see

AGUADA
18 km from Panjim, the site of the strongest *fort* (from 1612) in Goa. Situated on a headland of the Mandovi, effectively turned into an island by the Portuguese who linked the moat to the Nerul river. Its restored northern bastion now provides a harbour for local shipping, but some of the other bastions are crumbling. A beautiful 19th century *lighthouse* dominates the fortress area. The hotel within the grounds of the fort provides much tourist accommodation. The area is also the site of the Central Jail.

ANJUNA
Popular beach area. Adjacent to the headland of Chapora fort. In Anjuna is the magnificent *Albuquerque mansion*, built in the 1920s, flanked by octagonal towers and with attractive Mangalore tile roofs.

ARVELEM (ARVALEM)
9 km southeast of Bicholim town. 24 metre high waterfall, best viewed after the monsoons, and group of six *rock-cut sanctuaries*, probably of Buddhist origin in the 3rd–6th century AD but later given over to Shiva worship.

BONDLA FOREST
55 km from Panjim and some 15 km northeast of Ponda. A c.80 sq km wildlife sanctuary with mini zoos, deer park and natural habitat. Very suitable for children.

CABO RAJ NIWAS (KABO RAJ NIVAS)
Fortress (1540), now mostly ruined, which commanded the south headland of the Mandovi opposite Fort Aguada. The former *Franciscan monastery* (1594) has now become the official residence of the lieutenant-governor of Goa, an elegant mansion.

CABO DE RAMA (CAPE RAMA)
A ruined *fortress*, built before the arrival of the Portuguese, the most southerly of the Goan forts, and situated at two hour's walk from the nearest road, approximately 25 km south of Margao. Probably best viewed from the more relaxed vantage point of a boat.

CALANGUTE
The 11 km long beach of golden sand, which lies some 16 km northeast of Panjim across the Mandovi river, is known as the 'Queen' of Goa and is amongst the most popular. Both scenery and accommodation are accounted excellent. The beautiful *church* at Calangute itself has an artificial grotto facing it.

CHANDOR (CHANDAR)
Some 9 km east of Margao. The *Menes Braganza house*, mostly late 18th century and previously owned by the famous nationalist and journalist Luis de Menezes Braganza, has a series of magnificent rooms, especially the great salon with its fine furniture, and the largest private library in Goa.

CHAPORA

Fort on the southern headland of the Chapora river estuary. Built by the 'Adil Shah and known by him as Shapur, it is now ruined. The fort dominates Vagator beach, which is becoming increasingly popular, and is close to Anjuna beach.

COLVA (KOLVA)

One of the more southerly beaches and scenically excellent, with 40 kilometres of gently sloping white sand fringed with palm trees. It is 6 km west of and 10 minutes by bus from the town of Margao. The area of Colva village itself is favoured by local fishermen. Currently still relatively underdeveloped, although the object of interest for several tour companies. Approximately an hour's bus ride from Panjim.

COTIGAO

Wildlife sanctuary, in the far south of Goa. Less commercially developed than the other sanctuaries.

CURTORIM

9 km northeast of Margao. *St Alex* is one of the oldest churches in Goa, on the site of a Hindu shrine.

CURDI (KURDI)

10 km southeast of Sanguem. *Shiva temple* (11th–13th century), similar in style to the Shri Mahadeva although smaller and less well preserved.

DONA PAULA (DON PAOL)

Headland with a fine view of Zuari estuary and Marmagao harbour, approximately 7 km from Panjim.

GOA VELHA (PILAR)

About 11 km southeast of Panjim, on the supposed site of the ancient city of Gopakkapattana. *Pilar Monastery* (founded 1613), an important early religious centre and now an educational centre for Christian missionaries. Fine views can be had of Marmagao harbour and Zuari river from the hilltop. Relics from the former temple of Shiva which crowned the hill can now be seen in the Seminary. *St Andrew's Church* in Goa Velha is the starting point for the procession of saints during the Christian feast (see CHRISTIAN FESTIVALS).

GUIRIM

Just south of Mapuca. The *Souza Gonçalves house* has an unusual granite staircase and a chapel housing one of the few Gothic-style altar pieces in Goa.

KAVALEM (KAVLEM)

33 km from Panjim. The *Shri Shantadurga* temple is dedicated to the goddess who mediates between Vishnu and Shiva. The *gharbhakada*, or the holy of holies where the deity is kept, is especially beautiful.

KHANDEPAR

6 km northeast of Ponda town. *Khandeparker Hindu courtyard house*, built in 1890 and still owned by the family.

A short distance from Khandepar are 4 free-standing *rock-cut sanctuaries* dating probably from the 10th–11th centuries and the finest examples in Goa. Probably Buddhist in origin, they have finely carved temple spire roofs and interesting carved details, even down to pegs for hanging robes.

KUNDAI

3 km northwest of Mardol and 10 km northwest of Ponda. 250 year old *Sinai-Kundaiker Hindu family house*, with impressive rooms, fortified entrance hall and a series of unusual landscape and allegorical murals.

LOUTULIM (LOUTOLIM)

Near Raia, some 5 km northeast of Margao. Delightful *church* with single tower and a number of fine houses, like the *Roque Caetan Miranda* (1815) whose salon is particularly impressive. Just outside the village in their own grounds are the *Miranda house* (c.1700), with its splendid interior, and the *Salvador Costa house* which houses a wealth of fine furniture.

MAPUCA (MAPUSA)

13 km north of Panjim. Main town of Bardez Taluka. Busy trade centre. Weekly Friday fair and market, municipal gardens.

MARDOL

On the main route 7 km northwest of Ponda. *Temple* dedicated to Mahalsa. It possesses carvings which relate to the Shakti cult and a rare series of carvings of Vishnu, as well as a recent enormous brass Garuda pillar on the back of a turtle.

MARGAO (MADGAON)

33 km from Panjim, the main town of Salcete taluka. Commercial inland centre. Rail links to rest of India and Marmagao harbour. Parks, gardens, Portuguese colonial and ecclesiastical buildings, including the *Church of the Holy Spirit* (1564, rebuilt 1675) with its majestic classical facade and a central square with a series of fine town houses and a superb monumental cross. The 17th century *da Silva house*, called Seven Shoulders, is well known for its splendid furnishings and the 17th century *Vicente de João Figueiredo* house has a marvellous collection of Goan furniture.

MARMAGAO HARBOUR (MORMUGAO)

34 km from Panjim and 4 km from Vasco da Gama, this is one of the finest of natural ports along India's west coast. It is an important centre for maritime activity with passenger and cargo ships passing through here from all over the world.

MAYEM LAKE

35 km from Panjim and just over 1 km southwest of Bicholim. An ideal picnic spot and boating venue.

MIRAMAR (GASPAR DIAS)

Beach with soft sand and palm trees. Nearest beach to Panjim (c.2 km distant) and an extension from Panjim esplanade. Approximately a five-minute bus ride from the city.

MOLEM (MOLLEM)

In the east of Goa. Baghwan Mahaveer wildlife sanctuary with 240 sq km of forested slopes, noteworthy geographical features such as the spectacular Dudhsagar waterfalls and a rich abundance of bird life. Also includes elephant, leopard and deer. Approximately one and a half hours drive from Panjim. Cottages available for tourists.

NARVE (NAROA)

37 km from Panjim and 5 km southwest of Bicholim. *Temple of Shri Saptakoteshwara*, built in 1668, showing many European influences.

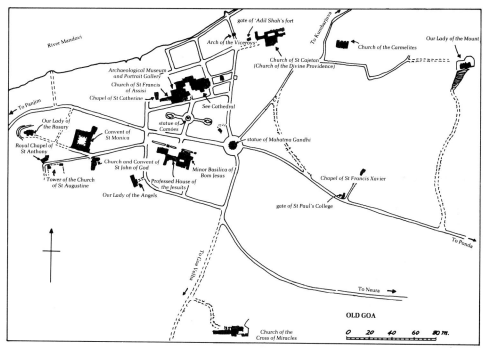

Old Goa, showing the principal monuments

OLD GOA (VELHA GOA)

Former capital of the Portuguese colony. Approximately 10 km east of Panjim and connected by a regular bus service. There is a wealth of Portuguese architectural remains to explore.

Old Goa's five main roads come to a natural focus in the centre of the great square where there now stands a modern statue of Mahatma Gandhi. Most of the buildings of interest are within a very short walking distance of this focal point.

On the road east towards Panjim is the *Minor Basilica of Bom Jesus* (1560), the church which houses the imperishable body of St Francis Xavier. Adjacent to this is the *Professed House of the Jesuits* (1589), now known as the Convent of Bom Jesus. *Our Lady of the Angels* is situated southwest of Bom Jesus, while directly to the east on the Holy Hill there is the *Church and Convent of St John of God* (1685) and almost opposite, on the right fork of the road, lies the *Convent of St Monica* (1607). The left fork leads to the *Royal Chapel of St Anthony* (early 17th century) and also to the highest point of the Holy Hill, where the Tower of the *Church of St Augustine* (completed 1602) is all that now remains of perhaps the biggest church in Goa. The right fork leads past St Monica to *Our Lady of the Rosary*, Goa's oldest remaining church (1543).

The road opposite Bom Jesus runs north past the modern statue of Camões towards the *See Cathedral* (1562), whose magnificent vaulted interior is worthy of a building intended to be the most important cathedral in the Portuguese Empire of the East. Adjacent to the Cathedral are the *Archaeological Museum and Portrait Gallery*, which houses a variety of Hindu sculptures and portraits of Goan governors, and the *Church of St Francis of Assisi* (1661), with its fine Manueline doorway, and then, at the eastern tip of the Museum, the *Chapel of St Catherine* (original c.1512, rebuilt 1952). The chapel was constructed as an act of thanks by Albuquerque for his victory over the Bijapur forces in 1510. To the northeast of the cathedral, on the road towards the Mandovi river, is the *Arch of the Viceroys* (rebuilt 1954), formerly a gate of 'Adil Shah's fort renovated by the Portuguese and used for the entrance of their governors into Goa. Another gate of the palace lies to the left of the roadway which runs east-northeast towards the well-maintained and splendidly Baroque *Church of St Cajetan* (c.1655), now the Church of the Divine Providence and a pastoral college for newly ordained priests.

Other buildings of architectural interest are more scattered, although no great distance from the centre. The ruined *Church of the Carmelites* is situated on a hill eastward from St Cajetan's just to the right of the road to Kumbarjuva, and still further east lies the crumbling chapel of *Our Lady of the Mount*, whose exposed position on the top of the hill at least has provided it with a certain resistance to the encroaching jungle. The *Chapel of St Francis Xavier* lies just southeast of the central square and north of the main road to Ponda. To the left of the roadway which leads to the chapel can be seen the only remaining gate of the important *St Paul's College* (1542). South from the central Gandhi statue towards Pilar is the *Church of the Cross of Miracles* (1619, rebuilt 1674).

PALOLEM (PALOLEN)
Just west of Chaudi. One of the most southerly beaches in Goa and relatively deserted, with a backdrop of the Western Ghats.

PANJIM (PANAJI)
City on the Mandovi, the capital of Goa. Originally a major port, although most operations have now shifted to Vasco, it still retains the old, narrow streets with their tavernas which lead down to the river. River esplanade and gardens, with Albuquerque memorial. Fish market. Shops are often behind pillared arcades and sheltered from the sun.

Interesting buildings include the 'Adil Shah palace, which is now the Secretariat, and the nearby 17th century *Mamai Kamat house*, home to a great extended family. There is also the *Dempo Hindu family house*, built in the 17th century. Although much of the house has been appropriated for other uses, the impressive verandah remains and the Dempo family still retain the daily tradition of feeding the needy. The *Church of Our Lady of the Immaculate Conception* is one of the oldest buildings in Panjim. Founded before 1541 and rebuilt in 1619, it is the focal point of the city's religious feasts. The great *Jama Masjid*, completely renovated in 1959 after its construction in the last century, is located in the middle of the city. In the district of Fontainhas can be found the important *Archives Museum of Goa, Daman and Diu*, as well as the *Chapel of St Sebastian*, built in 1888, which houses the crucifix originally used in the palace of the Inquisition in Old Goa.

PERNEM
14 km north of Mapuca, 28 km from Panjim. *Deshprabhu house*, perhaps the grandest house in Goa. Built in the 19th century, the facade conceals a complex of 16 extensive courtyards, one of which houses an interesting museum of Goan artifacts. Pernem's *Shri Bhagvati temple*, reputedly over 500 years old, has two life-size images of elephants either side of the entrance. Also noteworthy is the *Shri Shantadurga temple* in Dhargal, near Pernem.

PONDA
30 km southeast of Panjim. Main town of the district at an important junction of highways. Some industrial development. The *Safa Masjid* is the most famous of the mosques in Ponda. Constructed by Ibrahim 'Adil Shah in 1560.

PRIOL
22km from Panjim and on the northwest side of Ponda. *Temple of Shri Manguesh*, built in the sixteenth century and one of the most impressive temples in Goa. Painted white, it provides a magnificent contrast to the grove of green palms which surround it.

QUEULA
Just over 2 km west of Ponda town. *Temple of Shri Shantadurga* (1738), an important monument and, like many other Goan temples, strongly influenced by European architectural design.

RACHOL (RAIA or RAYA)
Some 5 km northeast of Margao. Although the great fort, which was one of the most ancient in Goa and originally in the possession of the Idalcan, has virtually disappeared, the *Seminary* (1580) remains and houses a famous library.

REIS MAGOS FORT
Built in 1551, facing Panjim across the Mandovi, the *fort* lies some 2.5 kilometres east of Fort Aguada, and was erected on the site of a Hindu temple. Its turreted walls are in perfect condition and house a local prison. It was a centre of the Franciscan Order and alongside its walls is one of the earliest churches in Goa.

RIVONA
Some 10 km southwest of Sanguem. *Cave complex*, probably used as living quarters for Buddhist monks and constructed around 7th century AD, before finally being converted for Hindu worship. Interesting architectural features.

SALIGAO
13 km northwest of Panjim. The *Church of the Rosary* is the only example of the Gothic style in the whole of the territory.

SANQUELIM
41 km from Panjim and 8 km southeast of Bicholim town. *Temple of Vitthala*, recently renovated, and in the North Indian style. Original carved wooden columns and a magnificent wooden temple cart. *Ranes house*, typical of the great Hindu family houses, with superbly carved columns.

SANTO ESTEVAM
This island is some 6 km south of Bicholim and is the site of the *fort* captured by the Marathas in 1683. It has a dry moat and its outer walls and main gate are still standing.

SHIRODA (SIRODA)
10 km south of Ponda. The impressive *temple of Shri Kamaxi*, dating back to the 16th century.

TALLAULI (TALAULIM)
11 km from Panjim and a few km southwest of Old Goa. *Church of St Anna*, a marvellous example of Indian Baroque architecture.

TAMBDI SURLA
65 km from Panjim, in the small town of Tambdi, within the confines of the Molem wildlife sanctuary and some 7 km north-northeast of Molem itself. The *Shri Mahadeva temple* is the only major specimen of Kadamba-Chalukyan architecture (12th–13th century) extant in Goa and boasts bas-reliefs of superb workmanship.

TERACOL (TIRACOL)
Site of a key Portuguese *fort* for the defence of Goa, on the north side of the estuary of the Teracol river, the most northerly boundary of Goa. Decorative turrets and dry moat with commanding views of the estuary and ocean. The church set in the middle of the fortress has a classical late Goan facade. The fort is at present used as a tourist hotel. The beach is situated at the confluence of river and sea and generally recognised for its tranquillity.

VAGATOR BEACH
Popular beach, dominated by Chapora fort to the north on its imposing headland. To the south of Vagator is Calangute Beach.

VASCO DA GAMA
30 km from Panjim, this is a large modern port, adjacent to Marmagao harbour. The airport is situated on the edge of the city. Passenger rail links to the rest of India.

BIBLIOGRAPHY

Alvares, Claude, 'Goa: Finished in Ten years', *Inside Outside*, Vol. 2, Bombay, 1979.

Beckingham, C.F., and Huntingford, G.W.B., *Some Records of Ethiopia 1593–1646*, Hakluyt Society, London, 1954.
    The Prester John of the Indies, Hakluyt Society, Cambridge, 1961.
Boxer, C.R., *The Portuguese Seaborne Empire: (1425–1825)*, London, 1965.
    From Lisbon to Goa, 1500–1750: Studies in Portuguese Maritime Enterprise, London, 1984.
Burton, Richard, *Goa and the Blue Mountains*, London, 1851.

Carswell, John, 'China and Islam: a Survey of the Coast of India and Ceylon', *Transactions of the Oriental Ceramic Society*, 1977–78, Volume 42.
Correia-Afonso, John, editor, *Indo-Portuguese History, Sources and Problems*, Bombay, 1981.
da Cruz, Antonio, *Goa—Men and Matters*, Goa, 1974.

Doshi, Dr Saryu, editor, *Goa: Cultural Patterns*, Bombay, 1983.

Esteves, Sarto, *Politics and Political Leadership in Goa*, New Delhi and Bangalore, 1986.

Gaitonde, P.D., *The Liberation of Goa: A Participant's View of History*, London and New York, 1987.
Gomes, Olivinho J.F., *Village Goa (A Study of Goan Social Structure and Change)*, New Delhi, 1987.
Gune, V.T., *Ancient Shrines of Goa: A Pictorial Survey*, Goa, 1965.

Kirkman, James, *Fort Jesus: A Portuguese Fortress on the East African Coast*, Oxford, 1974.

Macaulay, Rose, *Pleasure of Ruins*, London, 1964.
    India: A travel survival kit, Australia, 1981.
Majumdar, R.C., general editor, *The History and Culture of the Indian People*, Vols. 4, 5, 6 & 8, Bombay, 1955–1977.
Menezes Braganza, Biographical Sketch, Goa, 1972.
de Menezes, Antonio, *Goa—Historical Notes*, Vol. I, Goa, 1978.
Mitragotri, V.R., 'Rock cut sanctuaries of Khandepar (Goa)', *Journal of Archaeological Studies*, Vol. V, Mysore, 1980.
Miranda, Mario, *Goa with Love*, Goa, 1974.
Moraes, Dom, *A Family in Goa*, Goa, 1976.

Nunes, Judilia, *The Monuments in Old Goa*, Delhi, 1979.

Pereira, J., 'Shrines and Mansions of Goa', *Golden Goa*, Marg Publications, Bombay, 1980.
Pereira, Rui Gomes, *Goa, Hindu Temples and Deities*, Goa, 1978.

Pissurlenkar, Dr P.S., trans. P.R. Kakodar, *The Portuguese and the Marathas*, Bombay, 1975.

Rajagopalan, S., *Old Goa*, New Delhi: Archaeological Survey of India, 1975.
Richards, J.M., *Goa*, Delhi, 1982.

Sewell, Robert, *A Forgotten Empire*, London, 1900, New Delhi, 1970.
Sharma, M.H. Rama, edited by M.H. Gopal, *The History of the Vijayanagar Empire*, Bombay, 1978.
Souza, Teotonio R. de, *Medieval Goa: A socio-economic history*, New Delhi, 1979.

INDEX